P. W. Barlow

Kaipara

Experiences of a Settler in North New Zealand

P. W. Barlow
Kaipara
Experiences of a Settler in North New Zealand
ISBN/EAN: 9783337339081

Printed in Europe, USA, Canada, Australia, Japan

Cover: Foto ©Andreas Hilbeck / pixelio.de

More available books at **www.hansebooks.com**

KAIPARA

OR

EXPERIENCES OF A SETTLER IN NORTH NEW ZEALAND

Written and Illustrated

BY

P. W. BARLOW

SECOND EDITION.

LONDON
SAMPSON LOW, MARSTON, SEARLE, & RIVINGTON
LIMITED
St. Dunstan's House
FETTER LANE, FLEET STREET, E.C.
1889

Inscribed

TO

W. H. BARLOW, Esq., F.R.S.,
OF HIGH COMBE, OLD CHARLTON,

AS A TOKEN OF

DEEP RESPECT, GRATITUDE, AND AFFECTION,

BY HIS NEPHEW,

THE NARRATOR.

PREFACE.

THE fact that nothing has hitherto been published concerning life in this part of New Zealand from the pen of a *bona-fide* settler has induced me to write the following pages.

Before commencing the undertaking, I had been at considerable pains to satisfy myself of the truth of this fact, and naturally so, for it is the life-buoy I cling to as I take this, my first dip, in the sea of literature; it is my one excuse for troubling the public, and in it consists my hope that they will consent to be troubled.

I do not pretend to literary talent, and my highest ambition is to lay the true narrative of my experiences in New Zealand before the public in a readable form. If successful in doing this, I shall be content, and trust that my readers will be also.

Many books have been written describing colonial life in this and other parts, in some of which the writers have identified themselves with the characters in their stories; but these have invariably been the works of *visitors to the colony*, not *settlers in it*.

There is to my mind as much difference between the two experiences as there is between the experience of a *volunteer* and that of a *soldier of the line*, and it is on this account that I approach the public with some small degree of confidence, and venture to lay before my readers the experiences of a settler in North New Zealand.

THE NARRATOR.

MATAKOHE, KAIPARA,
PROVINCE OF AUCKLAND, NEW ZEALAND.

CONTENTS.

CHAP.		PAGE
I.	OUR ARRIVAL IN THE NEW COUNTRY	1
II.	AN AUCKLAND TABLE-D'HÔTE	7
III.	A CHAT ABOUT AUCKLAND	14
IV.	MORE ABOUT AUCKLAND	21
V.	MY FIRST RAILWAY JOURNEY	27
VI.	LIVING IN NEW ZEALAND	33
VII.	A PERILOUS JOURNEY	40
VIII.	THE "TERROR"	50
IX.	A SALE BY AUCTION	60
X.	THE FAITHLESS MARY ANN	66
XI.	MY INTRODUCTION TO KAIPARA	72
XII.	A WILD PIG HUNT	80
XIII.	PURCHASING LIVE-STOCK	88
XIV.	A COLONIAL BALL	102
XV.	THE FORESTS OF NORTH NEW ZEALAND	107
XVI.	THE LABOURING-MAN SETTLER	118
XVII.	KAIPARA FISH	125
XVIII.	GODWIT SHOOTING	135

CHAP.		PAGE
XIX.	THE KAURI GUMDIGGER	142
XX.	A STORY OF A BUSHRANGER	159
XXI.	SPORTS	166
XXII.	SYSTEM OF GOVERNMENT IN NEW ZEALAND	176
XXIII.	KAIPARA INSECTS	183
XXIV.	A MAORI WEDDING	194
XXV.	SYSTEM OF EDUCATION IN NEW ZEALAND	201
XXVI.	A MEETING OF THE COUNTY COUNCIL	206
XXVII.	CONCLUSION	212

KAIPARA.

CHAPTER I.

OUR ARRIVAL IN THE NEW COUNTRY.

On the second day of July 1883, in company with my wife, six children, a servant girl, and a full-rigged sailing ship—captain, mates, doctor, and crew included—I, the writer of this narrative, arrived at the port of Auckland.

Our voyage had occupied one hundred and six days, and every one concerned was mightily sick of it.

Myself and family and the doctor were the only occupants of the saloon, and as the latter had been ill for a considerable portion of the voyage, and the captain and myself were at loggerheads, things had not been quite so cheerful as they might have been. We had had more than our fair share of bad weather too: seven weeks of continuous gales, during which the ship had been more or less under water—or, as the mate put it, "had only come up to blow" occasionally—and our provisions had near run out, so it will readily be believed the prospect of once more treading dry land was hailed with delight by all.

I am a civil engineer by profession, and having for some time found it very difficult to obtain employment in the old country, rejoiced in the prospect of getting work in New Zealand in connection with a land company, who were the owners of a large tract of land—500,000 acres—situated as nearly as possible in the centre of the north island. This company had a board of directors in London, from one of whom—a friend of an uncle of mine—I had a very kind letter of introduction to the company's manager in New Zealand. My intention was to buy a few of the company's acres and build a house at the place where they were laying out a large town. Being the first in the field, and having such a good letter of introduction, as well as very fair testimonials, I felt confident of success.

However, to return to our ship. As soon as she anchored off the floating magazine to discharge her gunpowder, before coming alongside the wharf, I looked about for a means of

ARRIVAL IN THE NEW COUNTRY.

getting ashore, and was lucky enough to have a passage offered me in the steam launch which had brought the health officer on board.

My mind was too bent on discovering house-room for my family, to think much of anything else, though I must confess I was not impressed with my first view of Auckland. I walked up the main street and opened negotiations with some of the principal hotels, but these proving too expensive for my pocket, I wandered about hoping to come across a house with the familiar card "Apartments to let" displayed in the window. After a considerable wear of boot leather and temper without any satisfactory result, I entered a small hotel (by the way, every beer shop in New Zealand is an hotel) and besought information combined with a glass of ale and a biscuit.

Having ascertained the whereabouts of what I was assured was a *most* respectable boarding-house, I set out for the place, and presently found myself opposite to a wooden structure in H—— Street, which seemed to my unaccustomed eyes to be a cross between an undersized barn and a gipsy's caravan.

With hesitating hand I lifted the knocker, and my feeble rat-tap was after a considerable lapse of time responded to by a female of doubtful age, and still more doubtful appearance. To this lady—they are all ladies in New Zealand—I told my wants, and was graciously informed that she would undertake to accommodate my whole family for six pounds per week,—which, by the way, was about one half the sum demanded by the most moderate of the hotels. With a feeling of relief at the prospect of getting suitable quarters at last, in reply to her invitation I entered the house.

"This is where they has their meals," said my guide, with evident pride, as she opened a door on her left and disclosed a room looking for all the world like a skittle alley of unusually wide dimensions, with a long table down the middle of it. Not a vestige of carpet was there on the floor, which was far from clean, and sloped towards one corner. On both sides of the table were ranged a number of kitchen chairs, and these, with a sideboard bearing a strong resemblance to a varnished packing-case on end, completed the furniture.

In a voice feeble with emotion, I requested to be shown the sleeping apartments, and was conducted to the back yard, down each side of which stood a long weather-boarded shed with

ARRIVAL IN THE NEW COUNTRY.

six partitions in it; each divided portion being supplied with a window and a door, and forming a bedroom a little larger than a bathing-machine—which it internally greatly resembled. Three of these were placed at my disposal, and I hurried away in a cold perspiration, caused probably by the reflection, " Whatever will the wife say?"

It was getting late, and I was getting tired. "Shall I have another hunt," I debated, and sacrifice the pound the wily proprietress of the caravan and bathing-machine had insisted on my leaving as a deposit.

I knew we could not remain in the ship, as the stewards were discharged, and there was no one to attend to us. With a sigh I determined to stick to my bargain, and hurrying down to the wharf in Queen Street, secured the services of a waterman, and was soon alongside our erstwhile floating home. On reaching the deck, my wife immediately accosted me as follows:—

" Have you succeeded in getting rooms? The children have been *so* troublesome. They are longing to get on shore, and neither Mary Ann nor I can keep them quiet!"

I assured her that after an immense expenditure of leg power I had succeeded in arranging about quarters, and added—as a vision of the skittle alley and the bathing-machines flitted before me—that I doubted whether she would find them very comfortable.

"Oh! never fear, dear," she cheerfully rejoined. "After three months on board ship one ceases to be particular! All I long for is a bedroom with plenty of room to turn in."

Again a vision of the bathing-boxes arose, and I trembled.

CHAPTER II.

AN AUCKLAND TABLE D'HÔTE.

THE afternoon was closing in, so collecting the luggage required for immediate use, and locking the rest of our come-at-able belongings in our cabins, we made haste to get on board the same boat that had brought me out. My spirits had slightly revived, as it had occurred to me that very probably the caravan and its appurtenances would show to better advantage by gaslight.

Queen Street Wharf was soon reached, and having settled the waterman's claim, I hailed a cab, into which we all bundled, and in a short time found ourselves at our destination. Summoning the landlady, and requesting her to show my wife the sleeping apartments, I stayed behind to see to the luggage, and—I don't mind confessing—to allow her time to get over the first shock.

Entering our bedroom a little later with the

portmanteaus, I was greatly pleased and surprised to find my wife apparently reconciled to the surroundings, her only remark on the subject being that it was a queer-looking place, and not much bigger than our cabin. She was greatly puzzled as to whether she ought to change her dress for an evening one before appearing in the public room, but I emphatically assured her —having the skittle alley in my eye—that it was quite unnecessary, and we remained chatting until a tinkling bell announced that tea was served.

A strange scene awaited us on entering the eating shed. Some twelve or fourteen men— I beg pardon, gentlemen—and five ladies were seated on as many rough-looking kitchen chairs, busily engaged in attacking the comestibles placed before them.

A few—a very decided few—contented themselves with making the fork the medium of communication between their food and their mouths, but the greater majority used for this purpose both knives and forks with equal skill and success.

At our entrance they paused momentarily from their labour of love, and favoured us with grins which seemed to say, "What confounded idiots you are to come here." One lady of angular aspect, and with hair of the corkscrew type of architecture, smiled affably, however, and, reassured by her complacency, we seated ourselves at her end of the table.

The gentlemen, who, with three exceptions, sat in their shirt sleeves, were too deeply engrossed in the work before them to converse, and the clatter of knives and forks was for some time the only sound heard. We sat gazing at the scene, until a husky voice from behind demanded "Chops or 'am and eggs!" and recalled to our minds the object of our visit. Having decided in favour of chops, some black cindery looking bits of meat and bone were placed before us — resembling the delicious grilled chops of the London chop-house about as nearly as a bushman's stew resembles a *vol-au-vent à la financière*.

I managed to stay the pangs of hunger with the assistance of some hunches of stale bread, plates of which were ranged at intervals down the centre of the table. My poor wife, however, could scarcely eat anything. As soon as we decently could, for the coatless gentry were still at work, we retired to our rooms, both wife and self depressed in spirits, Mary

Ann sulky, and the children in a state of subdued mutiny.

"We will get out of this wretched hole to-morrow, so cheer up, dear," I exclaimed to my wife after a prolonged silence. "It's past seven o'clock now, and if you don't want me, I'll take a stroll down the town, and get something for supper."

Off I went, and soon reached Queen Street, the principal thoroughfare of the town, which, to my great surprise, I found in semi-darkness, the only places lighted up being the hotels and tobacconists' shops.

"No chance of getting anything for supper here," I thought, as I turned up a street which I concluded must lead back to H—— Street. I had not proceeded more than three hundred yards when I espied to my great joy a small shop with a blaze of light in the window, above which shone forth the legend "Oyster Saloon." With quickened step I approached, and peering in, beheld a remarkably neatly dressed and pretty young lady standing behind a little counter, and apparently fully occupied in doing nothing. On the counter stood some pickle bottles filled with extremely unpleasing-looking objects resembling large white slugs, while a heap of oysters with curiously corrugated shells were piled in one corner.

Entering the establishment, I requested in polite terms to be informed the price of oysters.

"A bob a bottle!" replied the ministering angel behind the counter.

"A bob a bottle!" I repeated. "May I ask if that's colonial for a shilling a dozen?"

"Oh! I see you're a new chum!" responded the young lady, in tones of mild contempt. "Well, oysters ain't sold here by the dozen; they are sold by the bottle! There are about four or five dozen, I reckon, in one of these!" indicating the bottles on the counter, with their revolting-looking contents.

"But are those really good to eat?" I stammered.

"Try them!" she replied, spooning from a bottle about a dozen on to a plate, and pushing it, together with a fork and a pepper-box, before me.

Screwing up my courage, I got one into my mouth, another quickly followed, and in a remarkably short space of time the plate was emptied.

"Capital! By Jove! I could not have believed they would be so good!" I exclaimed. "They don't, you must confess, look very tempting in those bottles?"

"Well, perhaps not," said the fair one; "but, you see, these oysters grow firm on the rocks, and they are easy to open when fixed there by tapping the back of the upper shell with a hammer, but are terrors to tackle when loose like those," pointing to the heap in the corner. "Besides," she continued, holding up a bottle, "they are so much more convenient like this. Why, you would want a hand-barrow to carry five dozen of them in their shells!"

"But how do you keep them fresh?" I demanded.

"Oh!" said my entertainer, "boys pick them fresh for us every day, and what are not sold are thrown away!"

Oh! ye epicures of London, with Whitstables at three and nine per dozen, and Colchesters at two and six, think on this—oysters pitched away daily, probably in hundreds, possibly in thousands! Grind your teeth with envy; but take my advice, stay where you are. You are not the sort for the colony, and living *isn't all oysters*.

However, to resume. The oysters were so good that I asked for more, and invited the young damsel to join me; but she declined, and asked, in the course of conversation, what hotel I was staying at.

I explained that, having a long family and a short purse, hotels were too expensive, and that we had that afternoon taken possession of a portion of a boarding-house in H—— Street, which said portion we had fully determined upon restoring to its owners on the morrow.

"Why not take apartments?" she rejoined.

"Apartments!" I almost yelled. "Why, I have been prowling about for the best part of the day trying my utmost to find some, but could not see a single house with a card in the window!"

"The idea! as if any lady would put a low card in her window," she sneered. "But if you want apartments, my ma has some to let, and I'll take you there, and introduce you, if you like."

With much joy I acquiesced in the proposal, and having settled my account, and procured a bottle of oysters for home consumption, we proceeded to the maternal residence.

CHAPTER III.

A CHAT ABOUT AUCKLAND.

THE interview with the maternal parent proved thoroughly satisfactory, as did the maternal parent herself,—an elderly lady, neatly dressed in black, with silver grey hair, and a face which, before old Father Time had placed his brand on it, must have been very pretty.

I promised to bring my " better half " in the morning to complete arrangements, and hurried home with my oysters, which with some difficulty I succeeded in persuading her to taste. Having once overcome her repugnance to their appearance, she enjoyed a good supper of them, with some bread and butter that I persuaded our hostess to let us have.

Supper over, I detailed my adventures of the evening, to my wife's great delight, and we shortly after retired to bed, but, alas! not to sleep. Before the drowsy god could exert his influence over us, an opposing agent stepped in, and we discovered to our horror that New Zealand numbered among her colonists certain nimble little creatures well known in the old country under the generic name of "Fleas;" the Maori name is "Mōrorohū," which, literally translated, means, I believe, "little stranger." They are supposed by some to represent the first importation of animal life that the English favoured Maoriland with.

Since their too successful introduction, an Acclimatisation Society has been established, and under its auspices many animals and birds of different kinds have been acclimatised. Rabbits and sparrows are, I believe, numbered among its earliest ventures. Within the last year a large number of ferrets, stoats, and weasels have been introduced by the Government to destroy the rabbits, which have proved too many for the settlers in the south island; and probably before long we shall hear of snakes being brought out to kill the sparrows.

What animal will be hit upon to destroy the stoats and weasels when their turn comes—and farmers in the localities where they have been set free already complain bitterly of them—I am at a loss to imagine, though I have no doubt the members of the Society, with the aid of a Natural History, will be able to solve the problem.

The notion possesses me that if the Society continues to flourish we shall eventually become a sort of sea-girt Zoological Garden, and possibly be able to advertise tiger-hunting among the attractions of the New Zealand of the future.

I trust my kind readers will pardon this digression, for which the "little strangers" and the sleeplessness accompanying their presence are responsible.

In the morning we rose ourselves unrefreshed, though the unwilling refreshers of many. After breakfast, which resembled in every particular the meal of the previous evening, with the exception that stale flounders took the place of ham and eggs, a final interview with our landlady was held, and proved of not so stormy a character as I had anticipated: it was brought to a successful conclusion—at any rate on the landlady's part—by the handing over of another golden sovereign. Her strong point in argument was that we had agreed to stay for a week, and therefore must pay for a week. This logical conclusion I found it impossible to shake until I produced the sovereign, which acted like oil on troubled waters.

A CHAT ABOUT AUCKLAND.

All difficulties being thereby overcome, we made haste to depart, and a cab shortly after deposited us and our luggage at our new quarters, with which my wife was much pleased.

The clauses in the agreement arrived at concerning them were as follows :—Entire and exclusive use of a sitting-room and three bedrooms furnished; attendance on us to devolve on Mary Ann; cooking to devolve on landlady; housekeeping to devolve on my wife; and lastly, but not least, the payments for the apartments— three guineas per week—to devolve on me.

Prior to leaving home I had given instructions to have my letters addressed to the Northern Club, Auckland, care of ——, Esquire, for whom I carried a letter of introduction; but anxious though I was to get home news, I had had hitherto no possible opportunity of going to look after them. Now the family were fairly housed, however, I hastened to relieve my anxiety, and found a couple of English letters awaiting me at the Club, which satisfied me that all was well with those dear to us in the old country. A good many of my letters, I learnt, had been forwarded to Cambridge to Mr. ——, who was staying there looking after the interests of the land company to which he was manager. I obtained his address, and sent him a wire stating our arrival, and requesting him to forward letters.

Having settled that business, I hastened down to the wharf to see what progress our ship—which was now alongside the Tee—had made in the unloading of her cargo.

I found the Tee heaped with cases already hoisted out of her capacious holds, though nothing of mine had as yet been disgorged. Having the keys of our cabins in my pocket, I decided to take out the things that were in them, and with the aid of a man and a hand truck they were safely conveyed to our rooms.

My time was now my own, and I went for a stroll.

Though not impressed with the appearance of Auckland itself, I thought the harbour and its natural surroundings remarkably pretty, yet lacking the grandeur of the Bay of Rio de Janeiro and other harbours I have seen. The formation of the land is curious, and gave me at first sight the idea of peaks which at one time had been bold, but which by some wonderful process had been either melted down into undulating mounds, or were in course of being melted down.

The peak on the isle of Rangitoto, which shelters the mouth of the harbour, Mount Eden, and numerous others, come under the latter description, while the north head and north shore generally come under the former. It was the north head that particularly attracted my attention as we first entered the harbour; it is shaped like a huge inverted basin, and is covered with grass. I can assure my readers that after one hundred and six days at sea the sight of that grassy mound was good, very good, and will never be forgotten.

The harbour called the Waitemata, opening on the east coast, is as a haven perfection; it is admirably sheltered, has sufficient capacity to hold half a dozen war squadrons, and is deep enough to allow the largest ship afloat to enter at dead low water and steam or sail right up to the Queen Street Wharf.

On its southern shore stands Auckland and its suburbs, and on its northern the town or suburb of Devonport.

Another harbour, the Manukan, opens on the west coast, and extends inland towards Auckland, leaving only a strip of land, in places not half a mile wide, between it and the waters of the Waitemata. It has unfortunately a bar, and is therefore not much used by vessels of large size. The construction of a canal joining the two harbours has been proposed, for what purpose is not clear, unless the projectors have some scheme for doing away with the Manukan bar, thus allowing ships to come straight through to Auckland from the west coast. It is not at all improbable, however, that the promoters desire to have the canal cut simply for *the fun of making the land north of Auckland an island.* Of course the money expended on the work will have to be borrowed, so what matters!

CHAPTER IV.

MORE ABOUT AUCKLAND.

The principal street in the city of Auckland, as my reader has been already told, is Queen Street, terminating seawards in the Queen Street Wharf.

It is not an imposing-looking thoroughfare. No indeed! and at the risk of catching it the next time I am down there, I repeat there is nothing imposing in it at all; neither the street, the houses, nor the tradesmen. There is little architectural beauty to be seen, and the shops have for the most part an unsubstantial appearance, particularly noticeable in the upper portion of the street. The lower, or wharf end, possesses some substantial-looking buildings of brick and stone, the most notable in 1883 being the post-office, the New Zealand Insurance Company's building, and the Bank of New Zealand.

The pavement on the left hand side for a considerable distance is sheltered by verandahs built from the upper part of the shop fronts, and extending as far as the roadway, where they are supported by cast-iron pillars. They form an agreeable protection from the sun, or from sudden showers of rain, and are remarkable as evincing an effort to study the public comfort—an effort very seldom made in New Zealand.

Since I landed in 1883 the town has undergone great improvements. A good-sized railway terminus now stands at the foot of Queen Street. Tramways run in all directions. A great many brick buildings, some five stories high, have been run up. The Auckland Freezing Company have erected very extensive premises of brick on ground reclaimed from the bay. An art gallery and public library, contained in a really handsome building, has been opened. *The Star* newspaper proprietor has built large new offices; and an arcade with shops almost rivalling in style and finish those of its elder brother in London—the Burlington—has lately been completed. On the north shore a magnificent graving dock is in course of construction, which will be able, when finished, to take in the largest ships afloat but two, viz., *The Great Eastern* and *The City of Rome*.

With the exception, perhaps, that the majority of the houses are of timber, Auckland may be said to resemble the ordinary run of colonial cities: it has an unusually fair share of churches and chapels of all denominations, and a still fairer share of public-houses—I ask pardon—hotels.

Of places of public amusement, with the exception of a dingy little theatre very seldom used, and a so-called opera-house where occasional performances take place, it has virtually none, and to this fact is undoubtedly to be ascribed the large amount of drunkenness that exists.

The vast number of places where drink can be obtained show what a brisk liquor trade is done; but if half these places were abolished, it would not, I believe, lessen the drunkenness by a single man. Gumdiggers, farmers, bushmen, fishermen, and all sorts and conditions of men frequent Auckland town when flush of money, and they *will* have some amusement! There are no music-halls, concert-rooms, or other places where they can go and smoke their pipes and enjoy themselves, therefore they fall back on the hotels.

It may be wrong and wicked, but it's human nature. As Dickens' immortal Squeers says,

"Natur's a rum un;" and all the head shakings and turning up of the eyes on the part of the pious won't alter the fact.

I was wrong, however, to say there are no places of amusement except the theatre and opera-house. There is one. It is called the "Sailor's Rest." Suppose (to use a colonialism) we put in an hour or two there.

After ascending a steep break-neck sort of stair-ladder erected in the back part of a shop, we stand in a large room hung about with flags. At one end is a stage, and scattered about are small tables, seated round which we see marines and blue-jackets from Her Majesty's ship lying in the harbour, fishermen, shop assistants, and working men of all sorts. They are chatting and playing at dominoes, draughts, and other games. Presently "order" is called from the stage, a lady takes her seat at the piano, which occupies one corner, and a gentleman comes forward, makes his bow, and sings a very good song to her accompaniment.

Another song follows, then a duet, inspired by which a marine and a blue-jacket volunteer a second duet, ascend the stage, and sing it capitally; another sailor follows with a comic song, a gumdigger gives a recitation, and so the evening wears away. The room is crammed, and in the back part near the stairs smoking is allowed, so the smoker is not deprived of half his evening's enjoyment.

Ladies, *real* Christian ladies—not "eye rollers" and "head shakers"—flit about ministering to the wants of their visitors. Coffee is served, and the proceedings close with a hymn, which I must confess sounds out of place after the comic songs, and I think would have been better omitted. By the time the audience have dispersed the hotels are closed.

How those hotel-keepers must *abominate* that flag-draped room up the back stairs! If there were a few more such places in Auckland it would mean *death to them*.

While on the subject of Auckland, let me say a few words about the shops and the shopkeepers. First the shops. One very noticeable feature in the majority of them is the absence of taste in the display of their contents; there is nothing to attract the eye, and however good the articles may be in themselves, they are seldom shown to advantage, but are huddled together in the window anyhow.

With regard to their attendants. In the larger shops you always find civility, but never any approach to servility: the shopman does not press you to purchase, but if you elect to do so, you may. It is a *quid pro quo* transaction, with no obligation on either side. In the inferior shops you too often miss the civility, and the proprietor appears to consider he is conferring a favour by allowing you to buy. No attempt, at any rate, is ever made to push a trade.

The same feeling which pervades the manly tradesman's breast appears also to influence the lodging-house and boarding-house owners. "*If you want any article you must come and ask if we've got it,*" and "*if you want apartments you must find out our address—we are not going to bother,*" are the sentiments which I fancy form the basis of the trading principles of the aristocratic tradesmen and lodging-house keepers of Auckland. The reader will perhaps recollect the trouble I had in trying to find rooms when we first arrived, and the awful place where I eventually deposited my family. Now that I am well acquainted with the town, I find there are plenty of nice apartments and boarding-houses, though it would be impossible for a stranger to discover them: if I were an Irishman, I'd say—he would require to be in Auckland a month before he arrived in order to do so.

CHAPTER V.

MY FIRST RAILWAY JOURNEY.

I OMITTED in the last chapter to state that Auckland possesses a hospital (perfect for its size), and some grand butchers' shops.

The hospital I have been all over, thanks to the courtesy of the resident physician, and I do not believe that for brightness, ventilation, and all other essentials, its wards are to be surpassed by those of any hospital in London. I trust my readers will not imagine by my speaking of the butchers' shops and the hospital in the same breath that I desire to indicate that these institutions have anything in common or are sympathetic.

With this explanation I will proceed to the butchers' shops. Meat is the principal feather in New Zealand's cap: it is the one really substantial cheap necessary of life, and New Zealanders have not forgotten to make the most of it. It is the bait that has been found most attractive in the immigrant fishery, and by the use of which the agent-general has landed the majority of the immigrants in this colony. The shops where it is sold are quite a feature in the town, and must on no account be neglected. They are very large—larger, I think, than any in London, with the exception perhaps of one belonging to Messrs. Spiers & Pond near Blackfriars Bridge. They are also very bright and clean looking, being lined throughout, ceiling and all, with white glazed tiles. On horizontal bars of bright steel suspended from the ceiling are hung the carcasses of sheep and bullocks in vast numbers, while legs and shoulders of mutton, sirloins of beef and other joints are disposed on tables projecting from the walls. They are without doubt the most killing-looking shops in Auckland.

The auction marts form another prominent feature in the town, and of these I will have something to say by-and-by; for the present I think I had better return to my own affairs.

The letters which had taken a trip to Cambridge (Waikato) had now returned, in company with one from Mr. ———, who informed me he would be in town in a day or two, and would call. We therefore had nothing to do till then but amuse ourselves.

MY FIRST RAILWAY JOURNEY.

A trip to Remuera, the prettiest suburb of Auckland, in an uncomfortable omnibus, occupied one day. On the next, as my wife wished to do shopping, I decided to find out what shooting was to be obtained in the neighbourhood, and in furtherance of that object entered the shop of one of the two gunsmiths in Queen Street and accosted its proprietor, from whom I learned that there was some grand curlew shooting to be had at Onehunga, a place about eight miles off, on the Manukan Harbour. I immediately determined to go there, and see if I could not make a bag. As I found Onehunga was to be reached by rail as well as omnibus, I decided to try the former, with a view principally to the saving of time; so taking my gun, cartridge belt, and game bag, I made, in colonial parlance, "tracks" for the station, and took ticket for Onehunga and back, the high charge made—half-a-crown—astonishing me considerably. I was fortunate in just catching a train, but not so lucky in my choice of compartments, for I discovered, after the train had given its preliminary jerk—a mode of progression peculiar to New Zealand railway trains—that the gentleman by my side was suffering from an injudicious application of alcohol.

The seats in New Zealand railway carriages run "fore and aft"—that is, lengthways—and when the first jerk came the afflicted gentleman toppled over against me, and I had some trouble in getting him fixed up perpendicularly again; the next jerk, however, found me prepared, and I met him half way, with a force that sent him over against his neighbour on the other side. This evidently did not meet with approbation, for he was shot back to me promptly, and we kept him going between us like an inverted pendulum. The "overcharged" individual operated upon took it perfectly quietly, evidently considering his oscillations quite the correct thing when travelling on a New Zealand railway. Playing battledore and shuttlecock with a drunken man is tiring work, however, and I was glad to change my seat at the first station we stopped at.

After three quarters of an hour of the roughest railway travelling I had ever experienced—progress being attained by a series of violent jerks—Onehunga was reached, and I descended and strolled away from the station, fully convinced that the railway authorities charged by time, not mileage; and this conviction I have since seen no reason to alter.

Onehunga is not an interesting port, and I

have no intention of describing it; suffice it to say that it is decidedly straggling. Going into an hotel near the station, I procured some lunch, and was directed to the most likely place for curlew. I laid up for them in some tall swamp grass, and waited patiently, but never saw a curlew all the afternoon, and what is more, have never seen one since I have been in New Zealand. I am positive there is not such a bird to be found in the colony, or, at any rate, in the province of Auckland; what are called curlew here are really godwit—the feathering of the two birds is almost identical, and both have long beaks, but the curlew's curve downwards and the godwit's upwards. The latter is a splendid bird for the table, while the curlew is scarcely worth the picking. I have shot dozens of them in the old country, and hundreds of godwits out here, so I ought to know.

I would not have wearied the reader with the above remarks had I not so often read in books, and more than once in newspapers out here, of the curlew in New Zealand.

When I reached the railway station, homeward bound, I had a long time to wait for a train, and walking up and down the dreary platform, I did not, no! I greatly fear I did not, bless that Queen Street gunsmith. The train arriving at last, I was jerked back to Auckland in an unenviable frame of mind.

The bag I made that day at Onehunga consisted of one king-fisher, which I looked on at the time as a great curiosity. I am wiser now, for they are the commonest bird we have in this part of the colony—commoner even than sparrows; but that Onehunga king-fisher I skinned and got stuffed, and that Onehunga king-fisher I still value highly. He is the first bird I ever shot in New Zealand, and he is the last bird I ever intend shooting at Onehunga.

CHAPTER VI.

LIVING IN NEW ZEALAND.

SUNDAY had now arrived—our first Sunday in Auckland. It is kept, as in England, as a day of rest, except by those unhappy individuals who are unfortunate enough to reside near a Salvation Army barracks! There is no rest or peace for them.

Early in the morning we heard the distant sound of martial music, and imagined that some volunteer corps was going to hold church parade; but as the sounds came nearer we were undeceived—no volunteer corps that ever existed would consent to march behind such ear-torturing noises. I hurried out and found that the disturbing sounds proceeded from the Salvation Army band. I am told that these Salvationists do a good deal of good: if they really help people to heaven with the awful apology for a band they at present possess, surely they would do a vast deal more good if they had better instruments and more practised bandsmen. The big drum, cornet, trombone, flute, and other instruments take a leading position in their ceremonial, and should therefore be put on a thoroughly efficient footing. If this were done, many persons who now rush away holding their ears when the Salvation Army band is heard approaching would stay, if only to listen to the music.

We attended service at St. Paul's Church, and had scarcely returned when Mr. —— called. We found him very gentlemanly and agreeable. He dined with us, spent the afternoon, and gave us a good deal of valuable advice. He said the roads were far too bad for my wife to think of going up country yet, and recommended my securing a house in Auckland for three or four months, and after seeing my family settled, that I myself should take a trip to the new township in order to see what I thought of it, and then make my final arrangements.

This advice appeared so sound that I determined to follow it implicitly. On Monday morning, therefore, I started out on a house hunt, and with little trouble succeeded in finding a suitable verandah cottage in the suburb of Parnell. My goods by this time were landed and stored in a warehouse near the wharf, so before our week was up at the lodgings I had them removed to our new home, in which we were soon comfortably installed.

Parnell is undoubtedly the aristocratic suburb of Auckland. It is as pretty as aristocratic, and I trust we sufficiently appreciated the honour of being the temporary possessors of a cottage within its precincts.

Several retired naval and military officers, and gentlemen from other of the recognised professions with small private incomes, reside there with their families, and form a society, agreeable, enjoyable, and exclusive. There is not the least doubt that New Zealand is a grand country for English people with certain tastes and private incomes of, say five or six hundred a year. I don't refer to those who are fond of theatre-going and such like vanities, or those who place cookery among the fine arts, for, as I have already hinted, New Zealand is no place for them. The persons I mean are the lovers of outdoor amusements, such as riding, sailing, fishing, and shooting, and those who like their rubber of whist, their chat and game of billiards at the Club, and their social, unceremonious evenings with their friends. The happy possessor of an income such as I have indicated could own a house in town and a place also in the country, where he might with his family pass the summer months; his country property need cost him nothing to keep up, for he would have no difficulty in finding a respectable working-man tenant, who, if allowed to live rent free and work the land, would not only look after the place and keep fences, &c., in repair, but would willingly keep his (the owner of the property's) horses in horse feed all the year.

If he selected the north Kaipara district, his property would be bordered by the inland sea, and he could keep his five-ton cutter sailing-boat, and enjoy the most delightful water excursions up the numberless beautiful creeks. A two-roomed shanty, costing about £30, would be ample accommodation for the working-man tenant.

But I can imagine my reader exclaiming, "Living must be much cheaper than in England to enable people with moderate competencies to thus have within their reach almost all the enjoyments which fall to the lot of rich county families?"

It is not so, however: the necessities of life, with a few exceptions, are on the contrary dearer in New Zealand than at home, but the out-of-door pleasures of life are *infinitely cheaper*. Small properties of twenty or thirty acres planted, fenced, and laid out in paddocks, orchards, &c., with a good six or seven roomed house, and outbuildings, can be bought for four or five hundred pounds; decent hacks to ride at from seven to ten pounds a piece; and a good second hand five-ton sailing-boat for between twenty and thirty pounds.

Children can be fairly well educated in the private schools of Auckland at far less cost than they can be in England.

In New Zealand it is not necessary to keep up the same style as in the old country — a man is not supposed to keep a wine cellar: he eschews top hats, kid gloves, &c.: his dress suit is more likely to deteriorate by moths than by wear: he lives plainly, and dresses so: his clothes which are too shabby for town he can wear out in the country—no one will think him one whit less a gentleman if he appears in trousers patched at the knees. Set dinner parties are not fashionable, though pot luck invitations are. To gentlemen and ladies who cannot enjoy their meal unless it is served *à la Russe*, I say—Stay where you are!—but to those who can enjoy a good plain dinner plainly put on the table, and are contented to drink with it a glass of ale or a cup of tea, the usual colonial beverage, and who are fond of outdoor amusements, I emphatically cry—Come! this is the country for you. You can have your town and country house—your horses and your sailing-boat, your fishing and shooting—and can save money. Ay! and invest it profitably too, if you keep your eyes open.

I trust the kind reader will excuse the foregoing outburst, and accept my assurance that I am not a tout for a land company. I am anything but in love with land companies now. But to resume.

My family being now in comfortable quarters, I started on my journey to "the town that was to be," in which all my hopes were centred.

The railway jerked me as far as the village of Hamilton, some eighty-six miles from Auckland, in a little over five hours and three-quarters, I having travelled *by the fast train*. From thence I was conveyed to Cambridge by coach, and was soon settled *pro tem* in a comfortable hotel. I had still thirty odd miles to travel, and had been puzzling my head all day long how to manage it, as I feared I should never find my way riding by myself; but here luck befriended me, for to my great delight I found a party of surveyors, four in number, staying at the hotel *en route* for the very place. I speedily made their acquaintance, and was informed they had hired for the journey a four-wheeled trap, called a buggy, and would be very glad to have me for a travelling companion, as they had a spare seat. I need scarcely say I joyfully accepted their kind offer, and we were soon on the most friendly terms.

CHAPTER VII.

A PERILOUS JOURNEY.

The news that greeted my ears the following morning on entering the breakfast room was that the all important buggy had arrived, and that we were to start as soon as possible in order to accomplish the journey by daylight. I made a hasty meal therefore, and was soon out inspecting the vehicle, in which, for the next seven or eight hours, we were to have so close an interest. It was a curious-looking affair, very like an overgrown goat chaise, with a sort of roof or covering supported on iron rods, and containing two seats, each capable of accommodating with moderate comfort three persons, while there was room for another beside the driver. To this arrangement on wheels two strong rough-looking horses were attached, and standing by their heads was the driver, a stout man with a short neck, a weather-beaten face, and a red nose of goodly proportions.

There was a good deal of luggage to stow away, consisting of portmanteaus, theodolites, chains, tents, &c., but at last everything was ready, and we started.

For the first three or four miles all went well, except the dust which went down our throats and up our noses, till we could scarcely breathe. This was not likely to last long, however, for black clouds had been rolling up since early morning, and hanging in the sky like regiments taking position on a parade ground before a review. A break up of the weather was evidently imminent, and we thought with satisfaction of our roof, and bade defiance to the elements. Soon the aspect of the country, which had hitherto been flat, began to change, and the character of the road began to change with it, the former becoming undulating and the latter uneven. As we advanced the country became more broken, and the road problematical, and at last we found ourselves travelling along a sideling cut in the face of a range of high precipitous hills, in the valley at the foot of which the river Waikato was rushing, roaring, and tumbling in its rocky bed. The road, if it could be dignified with the name, was scarcely twelve feet wide, and sloped in places considerably towards the outer edge, while two hundred feet below us rushed the river. In some places landslips had occurred, and it was barely wide enough for the wheels of our conveyance; and, to make matters worse, the threatened rain had commenced to fall in torrents, rendering the clayey soil as slippery as possible.

To say that the whole of the occupants of that buggy were not terribly nervous, would be to state a deliberate untruth. We all pretended to be quite at our ease, and I even tried to smoke a pipe, but our assumed composure was an utter fraud—indeed it was quite sufficient to see how we with one accord leant towards the hill, whenever the buggy wheel approached more nearly to the outer edge of the road, to be able to state positively that we were in a highly nervous condition. Old Jack, the driver, appeared to take things coolly enough; but he certainly had the best of it, for had the trap capsized he could have thrown himself off, while we, boxed up like sardines, must have gone over with it. He kept the horses going at a trot, wherever he could, and as they slid and stumbled onward, the blood-curdling thought would creep through my mind, that if one fell and slipped over the edge, he must drag us down with him. It was like a fearful nightmare, and the only reassuring feature—or features—in it was old Jack's imperturbable countenance, as he sucked at his short clay and "klucked" at his horses.

At last the agony was over; we were again on level ground; that awful rushing, roaring torrent had left us, and we breathed more freely. Old Jack now called a halt near a little brook to bait and water his horses, and we availed ourselves of the opportunity to dispose of the lunch—brought with us from the hotel—and began to converse again, a thing we had not thought of attempting to do for the last two hours or more.

I inquired of Jack whether accidents often occurred on the part of the road we had lately left, and he replied that he only knew of one waggon going over the edge—the two horses were killed and the waggon dashed to pieces, but the driver, by throwing himself off, escaped with a broken arm. He, however, believed there had been another bit of a smash or two, but did not know particulars.

Pushing forward again, we came to some extremely broken country, and old Jack's method of doing this portion, though it evinced a certain amount of knowledge of the laws of mechanics, was simply agonising. Whenever we came to a steep incline with a corresponding rise, he would whip up the horses in order to try and obtain sufficient impetus to take us up the other side, and down the incline we would go at a fearful pace, jolting, bumping, and hanging on like grim death. How the springs stood it is a marvel to me. We very nearly came to grief once, for the wheels on one side of our conveyance suddenly sunk in a soft bog, and it almost overturned. With our united efforts, however, we succeeded in extricating the machine, and resumed our journey, which at last came to an end, as we pulled up considerably after dark before the door of a little hotel—almost the only building to be seen in this future Chicago. Although our arrival appeared to be quite unexpected, the landlord and his wife seemed perfectly equal to the occasion. The buggy was expeditiously emptied of its contents, and bedrooms were promptly shown us. While we were engaged in removing the signs of the late fearful expedition, the sounds of frizzling and spluttering, and the delightful odours that reached our olfactory nerves from the culinary department, conveyed to our minds the satisfactory assurance that provision for our exhausted frames of no mean order was under way, and served to confirm my opinion that our host and hostess were *quite* equal to the occasion.

A hearty meal, followed by a pleasant chat, in a snug little sitting-room, with a bright coal fire burning in the grate, formed a most delightful close to what had been, to say the least of it, anything but a pleasant day's travelling.

I was up betimes in the morning, and was woefully disappointed with the look of the country. Stretching in all directions was a vast undulating plain covered with stunted brown fern—not a blade of grass, not a green tree nor shrub was to be seen—nothing but brown fern. The hotel, the manager's house, a wooden shanty, some surveyors' tents, and a small hut alone broke the monotony of the view. In the extreme distance could be discerned ranges of high hills, but whether covered with trees or vegetation of any kind they were too far off to determine. Nothing seemed to be stirring either; no busy workmen were there laying out the streets of the future city or erecting houses for the future citizens; no sign of anything going on. Nothing but brown fern. I had evidently arrived a quarter of a century too soon.

I will not say anything of the quality of the land. It may have been first rate—in fact, I am inclined to think it must have been—for on inquiry I found the company demanded eight pounds per acre for suburban allotments two miles from the centre of the township.

Nothing but brown fern.

To build the smallest house before a railway was made would cost seven hundred and fifty pounds, timber being twenty-five shillings per hundred feet. There was no wood for firing, and coals were eight pounds per ton. It was evidently no place for me, and the only thing left to determine was how to get back again. The landlord of the hotel, whom I consulted, told me that a waggon with stores and coal was expected in a day or two, and thought I would have no difficulty in arranging with the driver to go back in it. "To wait for the waggon," as the old refrain recommends, was therefore evidently the best way out of the difficulty, and I determined to do so. I called on the manager, and told him it would be impossible for me to settle there at present. He fully agreed with me, and advised my renting a small house in Cambridge until matters had become more advanced, when he promised to do all he could. He feared, however, it might be some time before he could be of any use to me, and I must say I feared so too. However, I thought it would be better to follow his advice, and determined on another house hunt when I reached Cambridge. I spent the rest of the day with him, and in the evening strolled back to the hotel, which was about three quarters of a mile off, being solely guided to it by its light, as there was no road or track of any kind.

On my way I was startled by hearing the most hideous noises at some distance from me, but gradually growing nearer. They evidently proceeded from human throats: what could it mean? Louder and louder grew the fearful sounds, until at last I could make out a party of men on horseback, who, on their nearer approach, I found to be Maoris. They passed me without notice, still keeping up the horrible din, and I came to the conclusion that they must have been imbibing too freely at the hotel. On arriving there, I mentioned the matter to the landlord, and he told me that they were natives from the King country who had come over to buy some stores, and that they were making the noises I heard to drive away "the Taipo," a sort of devil who devotes his attention exclusively to Maoris, over whom, however, he only possesses power at night. The Maoris, I learnt, would never go out singly after dark, and when they ventured in company, gave utterance to the unearthly cries I have described to keep him away; and it strikes me that if "the Taipo" has anything like a correct ear, the method adopted ought to be most effectual.

Two days passed, and on the afternoon of the third the waggon appeared. It had been detained on the road through a breakdown, and the driver had been obliged to spend a night in the open air, which, as the weather was now extremely cold, must have been anything but pleasant. He had succeeded in repairing damages in the morning, for, with a cautiousness begotten probably by previous catastrophes, he had with him the necessary tools, and was enabled to complete his journey. My proposal to accompany him on his return was favourably received, particularly as I agreed to pay a pound for the privilege, and on the following morning we started.

After over nine hours of torture, mental and bodily, for the waggon was innocent of springs, Cambridge was reached; and I was once more installed in the comfortable hotel there.

CHAPTER VIII.

THE "TERROR."

House hunting is not usually exciting sport, no matter how plentiful the game may be, and Cambridge I found very badly stocked. I travelled, I believe, over every inch of the scattered town, which has a population of about sixteen hundred, saw some places for sale, the prices asked being far beyond my purse, and inquired in almost every shop for houses to let, but without success.

I had almost given up in despair, when I struck what I thought was a good scent, which landed me in a shoemaker's shop, where I found the proprietor, a mild-looking, bald-headed little man, spectacled, and leather aproned, hammering away at a boot.

"I believe you have a small house to let?" I commenced.

"Well, I has and I hasn't!" the old man responded. "You see, I has a place, but it's got a tenant, and she's a queer 'un to deal with!"

"Well, you can't let your house twice over," I interrupted rather shortly, thinking the old fellow was making fun of me; "so there is an end to the matter!"

"Hold on a bit!" returned the patriarch. "I've given this here widder notice to quit, for I can't get no rent out of her, but lor! she don't care no more for notices than nothing at all!"

"But has she a lease?" I demanded.

"Lease indeed!" quoth the ancient one indignantly. "Cock *her* up with a lease! Why, she's only a weekly tenant, but, my word, she's a terror!"

"If she won't pay, there should be no difficulty in getting rid of her," I remarked.

"May be not! may be not!" he answered slowly, and in unconvinced tones; "but you don't know her. She's a terror! my word! she *is* a terror! But I tell you what," he continued, brightening up; "you go and say you heard she was going away, and you would like to see the place. I'll show you the way."

"Don't you think it would be better for you to see her yourself and arrange matters?" I queried.

"Me see her!—me arrange matters with her!" he screamed; "catch me at it. Me and the widder don't hit it at all, and she's a regler terror, she is. But you're all right though; she will be civil enough to you."

"Very well then," I reluctantly consented; and off we set for the abode of the formidable widow, and soon arrived before a little cottage with a piece of waste ground in front, shut off from the road by a hedge and a gate.

The shoemaker concealed himself behind the hedge, while I entered the gate and knocked at the cottage door, which was opened almost instantaneously by a tall, hard-featured, middle-aged female in a widow's cap. The door opened direct into the sitting-room, without the intervention of a hall or passage, and I was undoubtedly face to face with "the terror" herself. Fully sensible of my position, I raised my hat, and addressed her as follows:—

"I must ask pardon for my intrusion, but hearing that you were about to change your residence, I"——

"Change my ressidence! And may I make so bold as to hask who informed you I was going to change my res-si-dence?" she interrupted, tossing her head, and scornfully eyeing me.

"I understood so from your landlord this morning," I meekly responded.

"Oh! you did, did yer! Well, you can tell that bald-headed, goggling, mean little humbug of a cobbler that he's labouring under a miscomprehension!" With that the awful female banged the door in my face, and thus brought to an end my house-hunting in Cambridge. No sign of the cobbler could I see — he had evidently overheard "the terror's" concluding words and bolted.

I went back to my hotel dejected and out of spirits. On entering the reading-room, I found two gentlemen installed there—evidently new arrivals—who were smoking cigarettes and perusing newspapers. The younger one, a man of about thirty-five years of age, with a full beard and moustache, shortly after my entrance handed me the paper he had been studying, saying, "Perhaps you would like to see the *Auckland Star*, just arrived by the evening train."

I thanked him, and ran my eye over its columns. I did not take much interest in the New Zealand papers at that time, so was easily satisfied, and passed the paper on to the other occupant of the room, an elderly gentleman with a jovial countenance, whom the younger addressed as Doctor.

Acquaintances are soon made in New Zealand hotels, and in a very short time we were all three chatting as though we had known one another for months.

"Not long out from home?" questioned the bearded gentleman.

"Only landed in Auckland on the third of July," I responded.

"What do you think of the colony?" was the next question.

"Well, I hardly like to express an opinion yet, but I certainly am not favourably impressed with the part I have just come from," I rejoined, naming the locality, "and feel half inclined to go back to the old country."

"Your disappointment does not surprise me," returned my companion. "By Jove, sir, the way land companies and the banks have caused this part of the colony to be puffed up, has done more harm to New Zealand than anything else. I would not live here if they *gave* me a house. You can't go out without being choked with dust when the weather's dry, and there is positively nothing attractive in the whole place. Now, where I live, it is altogether different.

Beautiful country! virgin forests! an inland sea alive with fish—nice society—fishing, shooting, pig hunting, sailing—everything a man can wish for. It's a grand country—a *grand* country, sir. Ah! that is a place worth living in; but this—bah!" Here he paused to relight his cigarette, which in his enthusiasm he had allowed to go out.

Seizing the opportunity, I exclaimed—"I have no doubt it is all you describe, but I am a civil engineer, possessing very limited means, and anxious to get work, so fear it would never do for me."

"Never do for you—why not?" resumed my hairy interlocutor. "Far better chance of getting occupation there than you'll ever have here. Just where your chance lies. County Council got no proper engineer—you on the spot—make your application—produce your testimonials, and the thing's done. Tell you what—I am going up there in about a fortnight; you come up with me. I'll put you up and show you the country. Know a property that will just suit you—lovely place—dirt cheap, sir! Good house—orchards—beautiful views—grand, sir—grand!"

"What is the district called, and how far is it from Auckland?" I questioned.

"The Kaipara—the Eden of the north island, sir! and not more than ninety miles from Auckland—thirty by rail and sixty by steamer," replied my new acquaintance. "Delightful trip the water part. Don't think much of the railway part—never did like the railway—have too much of it perhaps—wretched accommodation—jerked and bumped nearly to death. Give me the water!" he proceeded enthusiastically. "Ah! when you've seen the Kaipara, you'll say it's lovely; I know you will. Take my advice, and come up with me!"

I thanked him for his kind offer, which I promised to take into serious consideration, and writing my Auckland address on my card, I asked him to call when he reached town, and I would then be prepared with an answer. He promised to do so, and at that moment the first bell ringing from the dining-room, warned us to get ready for the evening meal.

Having no further business to transact in Cambridge, I took the first train on the following morning for Auckland, which I reached in due course, and spent the evening detailing my adventures to my wife, and in consultation with her as to the best course for us to pursue. It seemed evident we must give up, at any rate for a time, the idea with which we left England, and it was equally clear that in order to live within my income I must buy a place with the few loose hundreds I had brought out, where I could keep a cow or two, and save rent, milk, and butter. I decided, therefore, to look at places that were for sale about Auckland so as to help me to come to a decision before my friend of the Cambridge hotel put in an appearance.

I had looked over one property at Cambridge, which comprised a six-roomed house, and eight acres of land. The house was in very bad condition—quite uninhabitable indeed; and for it and the eight acres I was asked one thousand pounds.

I saw several about Auckland, but could find nothing to suit me. My wife and I took a good many excursions together in this pursuit, but without avail. We also made some pleasure trips, one of which was to Mount Eden, lying directly behind the city. An easy ascent of between three and four hundred feet brought us to the lip of the crater, from which a magnificent view of the isthmus of Auckland and the surrounding country is to be obtained, the great number of volcanic cones visible forming a very remarkable feature in the landscape. They are, I believe, over sixty in number, and range in height from three hundred to nine hundred feet. No tradition exists among the Maoris of any eruption in the neighbourhood, though the fact that the Maori name for the highest peak, Rangitoto, means sky of blood, seems to imply that it has been active within their time.

The inside of the crater of Mount Eden resembles a funnel or inverted cone covered with grass and plentifully strewn with lumps of scoria. It is very symmetrical in shape, and one would almost fancy it an artificial creation. There is indeed plenty of evidence of the work of human hands on Mount Eden in the shape of remains of Maori fortifications, though the natural and the artificial are so blended together and softened by time that it is difficult to say where the one ends and the other begins.

When we had satisfied our appetites for landscape scenery, we descended the Mount, and spent some time examining the neighbourhood in the vain hope of tumbling across a place to be sold that would suit us. We were much struck with the elegant timber villa residences, surrounded by spacious verandahs, about which flowering creeping plants of various kinds, such as the yellow Banksian rose and the passion fruit with its splendid scarlet flower, climbed and hung in luxurious festoons. Some of the villas possessed gardens filled with beautiful flowers, including camelias, azaleas, spiræas, and many others only to be found in conservatories in England. Everywhere in the province of Auckland flowers of all kinds not only grow but flower most luxuriantly, and the lover of floriculture can indulge his hobby to the full.

CHAPTER IX.

A SALE BY AUCTION.

It does not often fall to my lot to do shopping—one reason being that my wife is fond of doing it herself, and another that I detest the occupation. It happened, however, a few mornings after our Mount Eden trip, that some mutton chops were required, and as I was going into the town, my wife asked me to purchase three or four. To avoid the possibility of forgetting my commission, I headed straight for the flashiest-looking butcher's shop in Queen Street, gave my order, and on receiving the chops handed half-a-crown to the shopman, who to my intense surprise returned me a two-shilling piece.

Four fine mutton chops for sixpence! Digest this information, my home readers, and then come out here if you like, and digest the three-halfpenny chops—they are every bit as good as English ones, and one-fifth of the money.

Strolling down Queen Street with my purchases done up in a neat parcel, I was nearly knocked over by a man who suddenly rushed out of a doorway with a gigantic bell in his hand, which he commenced ringing violently. "What is the matter now?" thought I. "Can this be an opposition form of religion to the Salvation Army, in which the bell takes the place of the drum?" Determining to fathom the mystery of the man with the bell, I stationed myself as near to him as possible without running a risk of being rendered deaf for life, and watched events. Nobody appeared to take much notice of the performance, but I saw people from time to time entering the doorway from which the bellringer had emerged. "No doubt," I thought, "some kind of service is about to be held;" and I determined when the bell stopped to form one of the congregation. People were now flocking in pretty fast, and the bellman showed symptoms of fatigue, though he stuck to his work with all the ardour of a religious fanatic. At last the bell conquered the man, and entering the doorway I found myself in a large and rather dark room, along one side of which all sorts of articles of furniture were arranged. On a small raised platform with a rail in front, to which a desk was attached, stood a gentleman whom I immediately saw was not a parson, but an auctioneer, for in his hand he carried his baton of office—a small ivory hammer. Round him were crowded about one hundred shabbily dressed persons, a large proportion of whom were Jews. Just as I entered the auctioneer rapped sharply with his mallet on the desk in front of him and spoke as follows:—

"Gentlemen, I have to-day to offer you some of the choicest articles of furniture that have ever come under my hammer, and I will but express the hope that you have brought with you plenty of money to buy with, and plenty of pluck to bid with, and proceed to business. Jim, move that chest of drawers forward, so that the gentlemen can see it. There, gentlemen, what do you say to that? a piece of furniture that would give a distinguished appearance to the meanest bedchamber—best cabinet-maker's work too. Shall we say five pounds for the chest of drawers? What, no bidders? Well, start it at what you like—say ten shillings for this magnificent piece of furniture—twelve shillings—fourteen shillings—one pound bid in two places—this remarkably handsome specimen of cabinetmaker's work going for one pound—twenty-five shillings bid," &c. &c., until it was finally knocked down for fifty shillings. The next thing disposed of was a clock, and then a sewing-machine was put up, which was just the thing I knew my wife wanted.

"Gentlemen," said the auctioneer, "the sewing-machine I now have to offer to you is the property of a widow lady in distressed circumstances. I will with your permission read a letter I received from her at the time the machine was forwarded to me, and I am confident that you will sympathise with this poor bereaved lady, who has not only had the misfortune to lose her husband, but is now, alas! about to lose her sewing-machine!" He then read the letter, the contents of which I have forgotten, though I recollect it stated that the machine was a "Wheeler and Wilson" in good order.

"Gentlemen," continued the auctioneer, "I am sure the letter I have just read must have excited feelings of compassion in each manly breast. Show it by bidding freely for the widow—or rather, I mean for the widow's sewing-machine. Shall we start it at a pound? What! no bid at a pound? Where are your bowels of compassion, gentlemen? Well, say ten shillings—ten shillings for a 'Wheeler and Wilson' sewing-machine—fifteen shillings for this splendid piece of mechanism—sixteen shillings offered—sixteen shillings for a beautiful widow's sewing-machine—seventeen shillings offered—eighteen shillings in two places for the widow—nineteen shillings—in perfect working order—one pound offered for this beautiful machine of a lone widow in good working order —one pound two and six offered—any advance on one pound two and six?"

"One pound five!" I shouted; and the second after down came the hammer, and the machine was my property. It was moved away by Jim into a little sideroom, and the auctioneer took down my name.

I went to inspect my purchase, and to my disgust found it would not move, and also discovered it was not a "Wheeler and Wilson" at all. Catching sight of Jim, who was no other than the performer on the bell, I said— "Look here, my man, this is not a 'Wheeler and Wilson' machine at all, and it is all rusty and won't work!"

"Can't help it, sir," replied Jim. "When you buys at auctions, you buys for weal or woe!"

"Oh! the wheel's right enough, and there is no question about the whoa," I sarcastically remarked, "for it won't move an inch; but I will not pay for it; it's not a 'Wheeler and Wilson,' as the auctioneer stated!" and in a state of righteous indignation I strode out of the place, leaving my chops unwittingly behind me.

There are eight or nine of these rooms, or marts, in Queen Street, and the system of selling all sorts of things daily by auction gives a sort of Cheap Jack air to the thoroughfare. Surely, if this method of disposing of goods of all descriptions is necessary to the happiness of the good citizens of Auckland, some side street might be selected in which the business could be carried on, and the peace and dignity of the principal thoroughfare in the city left undisturbed.

CHAPTER X.

THE FAITHLESS MARY ANN.

One evening, shortly after my adventures in the auction room, the servant girl we had brought from England with us asked my wife's permission to go out for an hour or two. This was readily granted, and no more was thought of the matter until ten o'clock came, and with it no sign of Mary Ann. She had promised to return by nine, and was usually fairly punctual. We sat up waiting until eleven, wondering what could have happened, and then, deciding to give her up for the night, retired to bed.

On the following morning there was still no sign of the girl, so I hurried down to the police station to ascertain if the inspector could assist me to obtain tidings of her. An interview with the sergeant in charge proved to me conclusively that Mary Ann as a speculation in servant girls was an utter failure, resulting in a dead loss to me of £50. He told me the police could do nothing unless a charge of a criminal nature was entered. I produced a document stamped at Somerset House, in which the girl agreed to remain in my service for three years at a specified rate of wages, on condition of my paying for her outfit and passage, and assured the sergeant that I had fulfilled my part of the agreement in every particular, giving her a most complete outfit and paying for a saloon passage. He, however, immediately floored my hopes in the document by telling me that no agreement of the kind signed in England was binding in the colony, and that to have made it so it should have been again signed before witnesses on reaching New Zealand.

"No doubt," he said, "your servant acquainted herself with this fact, and has run away in order to secure the high wages to be obtained in the colony, though possibly there may be a sweetheart in the case."

I assured him I did not think the latter at all likely, as one reason for her selection was her excessive plainness, which we considered sufficient to keep every man in New Zealand at a safe distance.

He remarked that she must indeed be a "rum 'un" to look at, if she could not find a chap in

New Zealand, for they weren't very particular; and regretting that he could not assist me, the interview came to an end, and I returned home in the hopes of learning some tidings there of the truant.

Nothing, however, had been heard of her, though my wife had made a discovery in connection with her box, which at first sight appeared full of clothes, a waterproof cloak lying at the top. On removing this cloak, however, pieces of sacking and old rags were disclosed, and proved its sole contents.

Mary Ann had evidently been taking away her things by degrees, carrying something away, probably, whenever she had had an evening out; and in case her box might be inspected, had kept it apparently full of things by stuffing in old rags under cover of the waterproof cloak. Oh! faithless Mary Ann. Your artfulness exceeded your ugliness, and our credulity exceeded both!

I trust the experience narrated above may be of use to persons bringing servant girls out from the old country, and will show the necessity of getting an agreement signed as soon as the colony is reached.

My readers will probably agree with me that

the New Zealand law as expounded by the police sergeant is a most absurd and one-sided one, placing the master altogether in the servant's hands, as he has to find the money for her passage, and probably, as in my case, for her outfit as well, while he has only her word to rely on in return. It is not, however, the only law in New Zealand that requires alteration.

We were now servantless, and until we could arrange about extraneous help it became necessary to investigate and to undertake those operations which comprise the duties of a general servant. My wife assumed of course the lead, and I seconded her to the best of my abilities—cooking, bed making, floor sweeping, chair dusting, fire lighting, potato peeling, and many other accomplishments of which up to that date we had had only a sort of vague conception, were now brought prominently under our notice, and became to us terrible realities.

I advertised in the *Herald* and *Star* newspapers for a servant girl, and several responded, but none proved suitable, the wages asked averaging from twelve to sixteen shillings per week. Two, but lately arrived in New Zealand, called together one morning. My wife interrogated them. Neither knew anything of cookery, could not wash, and had very dim notions of a housemaid's duties.

"Why, you could not have been getting more than eighteenpence a week each in England?" my wife exclaimed.

"Perhaps not," one of them returned impudently; "but we ain't come all this way across the sea for sich wages as them. We wants twelve shillings a week, and a hevening hout when we likes, and neither on us won't go nowhere for no less."

Further questioning after the delivery of this ultimatum was superfluous, and my wife hastened their departure.

Servant girls, or "helps," as they prefer to be called, have a nice time of it at present in New Zealand. They demand extortionate wages, and dictate almost entirely their own terms. No character is ever demanded when application for a situation is made; to ask for one would probably bring the interview to an abrupt end. Latterly, Lady Jervois, the wife of his Excellency the Governor, has shown a great interest in a capital institution called the "Girls' Friendly Society," with which none but girls of good character are connected; and if ladies would make up their minds only to take girls through this Society, a very different class of servants would eventually become established in New Zealand. We at last succeeded in securing the services of a married woman for the daytime only, and were again fairly comfortable.

CHAPTER XI.

MY INTRODUCTION TO KAIPARA.

ONE evening, about three weeks after my return from Cambridge, a hansom cab drew up at our door, and from it descended my bearded friend of the Cambridge hotel. I introduced him to my wife, to whom, when he was comfortably seated, with a refreshing beverage before him, he gave a glowing description of the Kaipara district.

"Ah!" he exclaimed, with fervour, "when the time comes, as come it surely will, when people will exercise their own judgments, and not be led away by flaming puffs in the newspapers, or by extravagant reports made in the interest of land companies, then the North Kaipara will assume its proper position in New Zealand, and be known throughout the length and breadth of the land as the Eden of the North! You think me over enthusiastic, no doubt; but wait until your husband has returned from his visit, and he will be just as enthusiastic as I am."

"But do you think he will be able to get work to do there?" questioned my wife.

"Could not have a better chance. Sure to drop into the county engineership. Just the man they want. Any amount of work to be done—bridges, roads, and that sort of thing to be made; and, by the by, I am going to start a fish-preserving industry—a grand scheme—thousands of pounds to be made at it; got hold of a German preparation that will preserve anything. Have a partner in the Waikato district who has arranged sale for any amount of fish down there. I'm taking up a lot of tubs and German preparation to the Kaipara with me. If you settle up there, I'll make your husband manager until county engineership turns up."

And so it was determined that I should spend a visit of a week's duration in the Northern Kaipara, and examine the property that was for sale. My portmanteau was therefore once more brought into requisition, and on the following Monday afternoon we took our seats in the train for Helensville, the terminus of the Northern line, from whence a steamer would convey us to our destination.

The railway journey was decidedly uninteresting, the line passing through some most dreary looking country, which became more uninviting as we neared Helensville, a township only impressive by its unsightliness. It stands on a river whose discoloured waters run between two banks of mud.

"Surely my bearded friend has been indulging in unlimited quantities of the colonial amusement known as 'gassing,'" I thought; and feeling very much tempted to return to Auckland, I expressed my opinion to my companion pretty freely.

"I fully expected some remarks of the kind —fully expected them," he replied. "That wretched journey to Helensville is in a great measure responsible for so little being known of the North Kaipara. People come up as far as here, and are so disgusted that they turn back. Wait, however, till we have crossed the Kaipara Harbour, and then give me your opinion. I fancy it will have undergone a change, sir. Yes; I *rather* fancy so. All I ask you is to wait."

We slept that night at an hotel near the railway station, and were aroused from our slumbers about three o'clock in the morning,

MY INTRODUCTION TO KAIPARA.

and told to "hurry up," as the boat was ready to start. After hasty ablutions, therefore, we struggled into our clothes, and speedily transferred ourselves to the deck of the *Kina*, a screw steamboat of fifty-three tons register, which was making noise enough with her horrible whistle and horn for a two thousand tonner.

We steamed away between the mud banks, which gradually widened out, and at last disappeared altogether as the Kaipara Harbour was reached. This we crossed in about two hours, and steered for one of the many armlets of this inland sea, which intersect the Kaipara district in so peculiar a manner.

The formation of the Northern Kaipara is indeed remarkable, and looks as though the land at some distant period had cracked and opened from the harbour in different directions, allowing the sea to rush in and form the beautiful creeks which everywhere abound. While crossing the harbour, my opinion, as prophesied by my companion and guide, began to undergo a change. The scenery there was very pretty; but when we were fairly in the armlet, which leads with many windings and turns to Pahi and Matakohe, I became thoroughly charmed. The virgin forests were there true enough—the native trees reaching to the very water's edge, with their hanging branches kissing its placid surface. Ferns in numberless variety—ranging from the gigantic tree fern with stem of twenty feet down to the dainty maiden hair, together with Nikan and cabbage palms—fringed the banks, and mingled with the darker green of the pohutukawa and other trees: at times bold grass-crowned bluffs of sand or lime stone met our view, giving place again to lovely little bays with bright shelly beaches and grassy slopes: ever and anon on either shore one caught glimpses of neat wooden houses, peeping out of nests of pine and gum trees, and surrounded by green fields of waving manuka—a background of high forest-covered hills completing the picture.

I was enraptured. After my recent experience of New Zealand scenery it appeared to me perfection, and I was prepared fully to indorse my companion's remark that the North Kaipara was a place worth living in.

The water teemed with fish, which were jumping in every direction, while birds of various kinds, including duck, teal, shags, eel-hawks, and flocks of godwit and red-shanked plover, added further life to the scene.

At last the township of Pahi—where my friend resided—was reached, and on the steamer mooring to the wharf we landed.

I was most hospitably entertained for a couple of days, and introduced to many of the settlers residing in the locality; and on the third day a visit to the gentleman with whom my companion had arranged I should spend a short time was undertaken. We left Pahi in a flat-bottomed punt, about fifteen feet long, painted black, and possessing an uncomfortable resemblance to a coffin with the lid off. The forward thwart, in which I noticed a split, was pierced for a mast; there was a seat about the centre of the boat for the rower, and another in the stern. Two large tubs and a package containing the German preserving preparation occupied the fore part of the cranky concern, while our portmanteaus were placed in the stern, and with a pair of sculls and a broken oar, to which a small sail was attached, completed the equipment. With some misgiving I stepped in, and we pushed off.

"Are you going to row?" I asked.

"Oh no, we'll sail—rowing is a waste of

labour when you've got any wind," replied my companion, as he adjusted the stump of the oar in the hole in the damaged thwart. "You sit on the weather gunwale to keep her trim, and we shall be across in no time," he continued, seating himself in the stern, and steering by means of a scull.

We found a pretty strong breeze blowing when we got well off the land, but the punt sat stiff enough with my weight on the weather gunwale, and we were going along at a grand rate, when an ominous crack was heard, and over went mast and sail on our lee-side as the damaged thwart gave way, whilst down went the weather gunwale with me on it. We did not upset, but we took in a good deal of water, and the bottom of my coat and a portion of my trousers were saturated. My friend, after an ineffectual attempt to reinstate the mast, applied himself to the oars, with the remark that "it was confounded bad luck," and in a short time we landed in a remarkably pretty bay with a white shelly beach.

My friend's friend, Mr. M——, was there to meet us, and received me most kindly, saying he was extremely happy to make my acquaintance, and hoped I would stay with him as long as I could. He promised to give me some fishing, flat fish spearing, and pig hunting, and to take me to see the property to be sold, which, it appeared, belonged to my bearded friend's brother-in-law. I thanked him heartily, and at the same time expressed my fear that I had been guilty of considerable coolness in thus taking his house by storm, adding, "My friend here, however, must share the blame with me."

"Oh! you don't know us up here, or you would never trouble your head about the matter: we're only too delighted to see you, and will do our utmost to make your visit an enjoyable one," returned my host; and thus commenced an agreeable acquaintance, which, I am happy to say, continues to the present time.

Following him up a steep path winding in and out among high bushes of New Zealand flax, cabbage palms, fir, acacia, peach, and loquat trees, the house was reached, at an elevation of some sixty feet above sea level, and I was speedily placed on a friendly footing with my host's family, which consisted of his wife, five children, and a governess.

In pleasant conversation the evening slipped away, and before we retired to rest, a programme, embracing a visit to the property for sale, a wild pig hunt, and a day's fishing, was drawn up.

CHAPTER XII.

A WILD PIG HUNT.

NEXT morning, after an ample, and, I may say, luxurious breakfast, pipes were lighted and a start made for the property to be inspected—distant about three quarters of a mile—to reach which another trip on the water had to be undertaken. A punt belonging to my host was got under weigh, and with two good men at the oars the journey was quickly accomplished, the latter part of our row being along a bank shaded by willow and other trees.

We landed on a limestone beach, and a sloping ascent covered with tall grass brought us to the house. It possessed six rooms, and a passage running the entire depth, terminating at each end with a door. The sitting-room and but one bedroom were lined and papered, and the rest of the house was only in a half finished state. A verandah ran round three sides of it, but part of the flooring was wanting: to make the house comfortable a considerable outlay was required. The outdoor portion of the property consisted of two orchards, containing together three hundred and sixty fruit trees. In one of them were a number of well-grown peach trees covered with blossom, together with some orange, lemon, and other sub-tropical trees. The second orchard—about two acres in extent—was filled with apple and plum trees three or four years old. A grass paddock of fifteen acres enclosed by a wire fence, a stockyard and pigsties, three or four acres of very pretty bush fenced in and bordered on one side by the water, and an acre or two of grass land about the house planted with ornamental trees and flowering shrubs of various kinds, completed the property, for which four hundred pounds was asked.

The view of the Kaipara from the verandah was lovely, and altogether I was extremely pleased with the place, though it was evident that the aid of a carpenter and painter would be required to make the house habitable. I determined, therefore, to think the matter over well and to ascertain the cost of completing the house before making any offer.

The inspection over, we returned in the punt,

and after lunch strolled over part of my host's farm of between four and five hundred acres. On the next day a pig hunt in the bush was arranged, in which Mr. C——, a sporting bachelor residing in the neighbourhood, was invited to participate. My bearded friend did not accompany us. We started about eleven in the morning, my host carrying a gun, Mr. C—— an axe and a butcher's knife, and myself a tomahawk. Three pig dogs—a breed, I think, between the bull and the collie—followed at our heels, and after walking about three quarters of a mile we entered the bush.

How comes it, I wonder, that the magnificent New Zealand forests are stigmatised with the name of "bush." If we turn to the dictionary we find that bush means a thick shrub. The forests here, however, are composed principally of gigantic trees, not thick shrubs, and to give them such an unworthy name is only. misleading. No scenery of the kind in any part of the world can excel in beauty the forests of New Zealand, and it is much to be deplored that they are not dignified with a more befitting title.

The ground where we stood was clothed with ferns and mosses in endless variety. Immense trees stood here and there, whose moss and fern-covered trunks rose to a height of sixty or seventy feet, and then broke into a crown of branches which met and interlaced overhead,

Heavy Bush, Matakohe.

forming a canopy through which the light of day but dimly penetrated.

Nikan palms, tree ferns, and small native

flowering trees grew between these giants, and from their branches hung clusters of lovely white clematis, bush lawyers, supplejacks, and other climbing plants. Although it was blowing freshly when we entered, not a breath of wind could now be felt, nor a sound heard, except the glorious deep note of the Tui—or parson bird—the harsh cry of the New Zealand parrot, and the gentle cooing of the pigeon. About us fluttered numbers of the bushman's little feathered friends—the fantails—spreading their large white fan-shaped tails as they darted hither and thither, and flew fearlessly within two feet of us. It seemed almost sacrilege to disturb the beautiful solemnity, but we had come to hunt wild pigs, and hunt them we must. My new sporting acquaintance was impatient, so away we went, the dogs heading us, and disappearing out of sight. We wandered on for some time in silence, listening for the dogs. At last one gave tongue, and we hastened in its direction; again the sound faintly rose, and shortly afterwards, further to our right, a distant noise of yelping, barking, and grunting reached our ears.

"Come along! they have got a pig bailed up!" cried Mr. C—— excitedly, as he plunged out of sight in the thick undergrowth, quickly followed by my host and myself.

I found rapid bush travelling by no means easy of accomplishment. At one moment my legs were caught in a supplejack, from which I would get clear, only to find myself firmly hooked by the claw-shaped thorns of the bush lawyer; then after a desperate struggle and many scratches would escape from its clutches, to become entangled the next minute in a bunch of Mangi-mangi, a fine wiry-stemmed creeper, which hangs in clusters from the trees.

I ascertained afterwards that my companions carried pocket knives, and cut away the obstacles as they presented themselves. Being heavily handicapped by my inexperience, I arrived at the scene of action a bad third, though in time to see the *coup-de-grâce* given by my host to a small pig which one of the dogs had seized by the ear while the other two were barking a chorus of approval.

The animal being pronounced a good subject for discussion at the dinner table, was dressed on the spot by my two companions, and hung up in a tree with a piece of flax—a capital substitute for a rope—to await our return. A fresh start was then made, and the raid against the pigs prosecuted with vigour. The dogs seemed delighted with their success, and anxious to secure fresh laurels. In a short time a more open part of the forest was reached, and here the dogs started three large boars, which came tearing through the trees with bristles erect. A bullet from my host's gun slightly wounded one of them, and he turned and charged towards us, grinding his tusks in his rage. To reach us he had to cross a small gully with steep banks, and this he was no sooner in than a dog had him by each ear. He succeeded in ripping one, but the other held on bravely, and a crack on the head with the tomahawk finished the boar's career. He was too big and coarse for eating, so we left his body where it fell, and satisfied with our sport, turned for home, carrying to the edge of the bush the carcass of our first victim, which we tied on a fence, and our host on reaching the house sent his man back with a horse to bring it on.

The last day of my visit was devoted to fishing. My bearded friend assumed command, and under his direction a fire was lit early in the morning beneath a large copper boiler; a certain proportion of the preserving powder was introduced in the water with which the copper was filled, and the mixture allowed to boil, while we sallied forth to catch the fish.

A net about one hundred yards long was produced by my host, and laid in the punt, together with two stakes to fasten the ends in the mud. We put off, and in a couple of hours had captured over a hundred fine mullet, and as these were sufficient to fill the two tubs, the net was hauled up, and we returned to the shore. The fish were then packed in the tubs, the heads fitted on, and the preserving preparation poured over them through holes afterwards plugged with corks.

The success of the day's fishing decided me to make an offer for the property I had inspected, and I finally agreed to purchase— a reduction being made on account of the unfinished state of the house.

Having arranged with a local carpenter to do the necessary work, I returned to Auckland quite satisfied with my investment.

CHAPTER XIII.

PURCHASING LIVE-STOCK.

I WILL not weary the reader with an account of our journey from Auckland to our new property. As soon as I heard that the house was ready for occupation, we bade adieu to Parnell, and after a somewhat tedious journey arrived at the Matakohe Wharf, where a large barge with two men in it awaited us. Into it all our goods and chattels, together with ourselves, some fowls, and a retriever pup, were stowed, and after half an hour's pull we disembarked on the limestone beach in front of our new dwelling.

The carpenter who had been doing up the house had secured for us the services of a country girl, who, among other accomplishments, understood the arts of milking and butter making.

My first care was to purchase a couple of quiet cows.

One I bought from a sanctimonious individual, who assured me the animal was perfectly docile, stating as a proof that his little daughter was accustomed to milk her. Having sold me the cow, he expressed himself anxious as to my spiritual welfare, and preached me a short sermon in atrocious English on the subject of his own righteousness.

Although the man was leaving the neighbourhood, I felt no hesitation in taking his word about the amiability of the cow—he seemed so oppressively pious. She was turned into my paddock, and in a few days one of my little boys came running breathlessly to me to say that she had a calf.

I had been advised, when this event took place, to immediately take the calf away, and I accordingly proceeded to the paddock to do so, never anticipating any difficulty in the matter. To my surprise and alarm, however, when I got within about fifty yards of the animal, she suddenly lowered her head, and came straight for me, her rapid movements necessitating on my part a most ignominious and hasty retreat. On reaching safely the other side of the fence, I considered the matter over, and coming to the conclusion that my new "chumminess" in the matter of cows and calves must be to blame, sent to request the assistance of a settler living near. He was unfortunately out at the time, but a lad who was lodging with him said he would come down.

On his arrival he inquired in supremely contemptuous tones, "What! can't yer take a calf away?"

The Pious Man's Cow.

I replied that the mother had protested in so very forcible a manner against my interfering with her infant that I thought I must have gone the wrong way to work, and asked him if *he* could undertake the business.

To this he briefly responded, "Rather!" and marched off with a confident air to the scene of action, while I secured a vantage place outside the fence. No sooner, however, did the pious man's late cow catch sight of the would-be abductor, than she charged like a 'streak of lightning, and I don't believe that that—alas! no-longer-confident—youth ever before made such good use of his legs. When he was in safety, and had recovered breath enough to speak, he gasped out, "If that there cow belonged to me, I'd shoot her!" and strode off without another word, leaving me in the depths of despair.

Later in the day, the labouring man I had first sent for—a solemn-looking individual, with a long beard—came down, and when I related what had occurred, said with a placid and re-assuring smile that he would soon settle matters satisfactorily. Procuring a tea-tree stake about five feet long, he requested me to follow him into the paddock, and on the way laid down a plan of attack.

"When I see's a propitchus oppertunity," said he, "I'll con-fūs-cate the calf; and if the parent animȳle precipices herself on me, as in all probableness she will, you must fetch her a right down preponderating blow atween the horns with this here tea-tree stake!"

I did not like my allotted portion of this elegantly worded programme at all, and suggested that I should do the abduction part, while he "preponderated" the cow. This being agreed to, we cautiously entered the arena, and seizing my opportunity—and the calf at the same time—I retired at a speed that would have completely shamed a New Zealand express train. I never attempted to look round, but I heard a blow and a dull thud close behind, and knew something had happened.

When outside the post and rail fence with my burden I breathed once more, and was delighted to see the settler standing triumphant, stake in hand, and the cow struggling on the ground. He had "preponderated" her in the most approved style, and the business was satisfactorily accomplished.

I thanked him warmly; and foreseeing that a difficulty would probably arise in the milking of the brute, arranged with him to perform that office for a time. It was well I did so, for she proved a perfect "terror."

To milk her it was not only necessary to put her in the bail—an arrangement which secures the head of the cow in somewhat the same manner as some of the old-fashioned instruments of punishment used to secure the head of a man—but it was also necessary to rope both her hind legs to prevent her from kicking. These operations had to be gone through night and morning, and caused a great deal of trouble and waste of time.

No more pious men's cows for me.

The vendor of the other animal did not pretend to possess any excessive amount of spirituality, and the cow turned out a splendid animal.

I next directed my attention to horseflesh, as I found it impossible to get about on foot to see the country. I tried several animals, but could find none in the neighbourhood to suit my fancy.

One evening a man rode in who was anxious to sell the quadruped he bestrode—a weedy-looking, weak-necked animal, standing about fourteen hands, decidedly shaky about the knees, and with a swelling on the off-stifle joint.

"There's a 'oss for you," he began, "choke full of spirits. Just the animal to suit yer. A regler gentleman's 'oss he is, and no mistake."

I remarked that I feared he would hardly be up to my weight.

"Not up to your weight! Lor' bless you, he'd carry you like a bird—'e's all 'art, 'e is. My word, you should see 'im junk—'e'd junk a brick wall down, 'e would."

I had never before come across the word

"junk" in connection with equine accomplishments, but presumed it to be synonymous with "buck," and expressed a wish to see the performance.

"Ketch hold of these 'ere eggs then," said he, handing me a basket. He next proceeded to cut a switch, armed with which he remounted the "junker," and pulling hard at the reins with one hand, punished the unfortunate animal with the switch, at the same time digging the spurs well home.

After pursuing these tactics for a short time, he looked over his shoulder at me and questioned, "Ain't 'e junking yet?"

"No," I replied, not liking to confess ignorance of the term; "he does not seem to be 'junking' much."

Another and a heavier dose of whip and spur torture was then administered, and at last the unhappy quadruped gave a feeble shake with one hind leg.

"He's junking now a bit, I think," I cried, anxious to stop the exhibition.

"Oh! that ain't nothink," replied the owner. "Lor' bless you, you should see 'im junk sometimes; he'd junk a brick wall, 'e would; but 'e ain't in spirits now."

The latter fact I was fully prepared to corroborate, and may add that I did *not* purchase the "junker."

I eventually succeeded in getting suited, and was able to look about the country.

The tremendously steep grades on the so-called roads astonished me very much, but the horses bred out here think nothing of them. In the winter time these roads are veritable bogs in some places, and travelling is then anything but pleasant. When they become slippery, the horses have a fashion of putting their feet together, throwing themselves well back on their haunches, and sliding down the steep inclines. They never come to grief, and all the rider has to do is to lean well back in the saddle.

The main road through the county is supposed to be constructed by the local governing body, called the County Council, which is composed of representatives from the several ridings or districts forming the county, each riding electing a councillor every three years.

Too often the sole aim of a councillor is to get as much done as possible for the road near his own house, and to secure as much compensation as he can for himself and his friends, therefore almost useless roads are frequently promoted, and the money frittered away in their construction and in compensation to the owners of the land through which they pass.

The main county road here is not yet formed in places, and though large sums have been expended, there was very little in the way of solid, substantial work to be seen until the last few months. Matakohe belonged to the Hobson County Council, which has existed for over ten years; it now forms part of a new county called the Otamatea.

County Councils have power to levy rates and taxes, and to borrow money from the Government under certain conditions, and they take care to exercise all their privileges in these respects.

When the chairman of a County Council is a large employer of labour and a man of influence, his part of the county generally shows the best graded and best metalled roads. Besides the County Councils, many of the ridings—of which Matakohe is one—possess Road Boards, also empowered to levy rates, and with the money carry out works on branch roads.

It is very commonly believed that the country would progress far more rapidly if County Councils were abolished and the different districts represented solely by Road

Boards, which would determine the works considered most desirable, and draw up half yearly reports to be laid before a Government engineer, who, after examining into the merits of the schemes proposed, would finally decide on those most likely to be beneficial to the county, and which could be undertaken with the funds in hand.

Enough, however, for the present of County Councils. The Matakoheans can certainly have no wish to uphold the system, as very little indeed has been done for their district by the county to which it, until quite lately, belonged. Its misfortune in this respect may have been due to its *situation;* it certainly was not due to its size, for Matakohe formed one of the largest ridings in the county.

It boasts of between forty and fifty private houses scattered over a somewhat large area; a good-sized public hall where concerts, tea and prayer meetings, dances and theatrical performances are held from time to time; a chapel used on alternate Sundays by the Wesleyans and Church of England people; a cemetery, a Government school-house, a public library, &c. &c.; three general stores (or shops, as they would be called in England); a saw-mill, a tremendously long wharf in a tremendously inconvenient place, and a capital racecourse, where the Matakohe Racing Club holds an annual meeting.

Horse-racing is one of the great national amusements of New Zealanders, and there are very few settlements in the Northern Kaipara which do not number owners of racehorses among their inhabitants.

In England racing is associated with betting, blacklegs, welshers, suicides, and other disagreeable things: out here, as far as small country meetings are concerned, it means genuine, honest, legitimate sport, and should be encouraged, as calculated to improve the breed of horses in the colony, and to do a great amount of good to the districts in which the meetings are held.

A sort of betting-machine called the "Totalisator" has indeed been legalised by the New Zealand Government, but may only be used at race meetings where prizes of thirty pounds and upwards are given. It therefore does not affect in any way small meetings like ours, and the Matakohe Racing Club have no desire that it should.

For the benefit of my readers who are unacquainted with the betting-machine, I will endeavour to describe the manner in which it is worked. The intending speculator enters a small office and buys his ticket, or tickets, according to his rashness, and then proceeds to examine a board on one of the walls of an inner chamber, where are displayed certain variable numbers arranged in the following manner :—

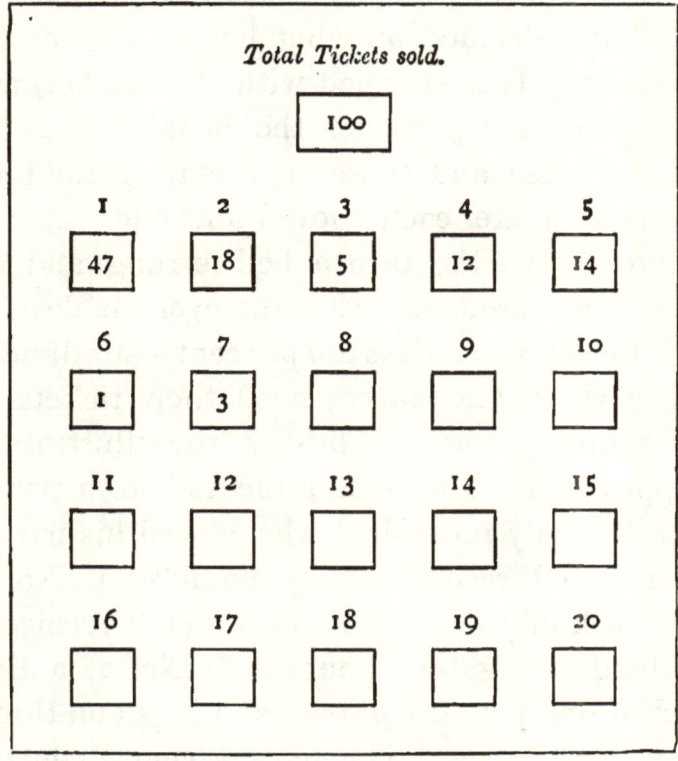

The numbers 1, 2, 3, 4, 5, 6, 7, represent the

starting horses in the order shown on the Racing Club's card. They may therefore be taken to stand instead of the horses' names.

In the illustration above seven horses are supposed to be going to run. The numerals underneath in the squares indicate the number of tickets invested on each horse, and the top square records the total tickets sold.

When the investor has consulted his "correct card," and decided on what horse to place his ticket, he gets it stamped with its number, and the figure or figures on the board under the selected horse and those representing the total tickets sold are each moved on one. A few minutes before the race a bell is rung, and the totalisator closed, and after the event is decided the total proceeds—less ten per cent.—are divided among those who have placed their tickets on the winning horse. Thus in the illustration, supposing No. 6 won, and the tickets a pound each, the wily individual who placed his money there would receive ninety pounds; if No. 3 won, each of the five investors would receive a dividend of eighteen pounds; if No. 1, a dividend of one pound eighteen shillings and threepence, and so on. The ten per cent. deducted from the receipts is divided between the proprietors of the machine and the Jockey Club; and inasmuch as fourteen or fifteen thousand pounds generally passes through it at one of the large Racing Club Meetings, the totalisator will be seen to be a paying concern. The advisability of taxing it was mooted in Parliament last year; and as our sage administrators of the law have deemed it right to make the betting-machine legal, surely they cannot be wrong in taxing it heavily as a luxury.

CHAPTER XIV.

A COLONIAL BALL.

We had not been long settled in Matakohe when an invitation to a ball at Mr. M——'s was received, asking us to go early in the day, as the tide then suited best, to bring our evening clothes with us, and to dress there. We accomplished the journey in my punt, for I had by this time one of my own, and on our arrival at Mr. M——'s found the household very busy with preparations.

One half the spacious verandah had been closed in with canvas, and formed a supper room. It was decorated with flags, Nikau palms, ferns, and flowers with very pretty effect. The other half was to be utilised as a promenade, and was hung with Chinese lanterns.

As the afternoon advanced, guests began to arrive—some on horseback, and some by boat. They all brought their evening clothes with them, not in portmanteaus, but in *flour bags*.

It is most surprising to a new chum to see the manifold uses to which flour bags are put to here. Besides usually taking the place of portmanteaus, they are made into aprons, kitchen cloths, dusters, and sometimes even into trousers for boys. Not long ago I met a lad with a pair on. On one leg, printed in large red letters, was "Wood silk dressed;" and on the other "Lamb's Superfine." Almost every one bakes at home in the country, so flour bags are very plentiful.

Rather late in the afternoon a gentleman arrived in a punt with his wife. It was nearly low water, and he got stranded in the mud fully a quarter of a mile from the beach. Finding he could not get the punt any further, he jumped overboard—sinking immediately nearly up to his waist—and pushed the punt with his wife in it to the shore. Changing his clothes in a boathouse on the beach, he shortly after appeared at the house as though nothing unusual had occurred, and I don't think considered his adventure worthy of mention to any one.

I have had several mud-larking experiences myself since then, but have not yet learned to behave with the *sang froid* displayed by the gentleman on this occasion.

When the time arrived for donning our dress clothes, I was ushered into a huge barn standing close to the house, where several washing basins, brushes and combs, looking-glasses and other toilet necessaries had been placed in position on tables and boxes. Between thirty and forty gentlemen, in various stages of dressing, were there, and jokes and repartee were being bandied about freely. Several of the gentlemen caricatured in that amusing book, "Brighter Britain,"—written after a visit of the author to this part of the colony,—were present, and most of them had already called and made my acquaintance.

The feat of dressing accomplished, and having succeeded in arranging my tie in some sort of fashion by the aid of a hand-glass and flickering candle, I proceeded to the drawing-room, from whence already issued the enlivening strains of one of Godfrey's valses.

The settlers up here, and in the province of Auckland generally, are most enthusiastic about dancing. Young and old, married and single, all delight in it, and no opportunity of indulging in a dance is ever neglected.

Flirtation I have never seen attempted, and conversation indeed is only sparsely carried on.

It is in the dancing itself that the enjoyment is centred, and to it the attention of both ladies and gentlemen is almost wholly directed. An anxious expression is ofttimes observable on the face of a male performer, as though his whole mind was concentrated in the effort to acquit himself well in the task before him; but though his countenance depicts no pleasurable emotion, he doubtless enjoys himself immensely.

On the present occasion dancing was carried on with unrelaxed vigour until past midnight, when a move was made to the supper room. The inner man refreshed, dancing was resumed, and day began to dawn before the party broke up.

The greater part of the ladies slept at the house, though some rode straight away after donning their riding-habits. The gentlemen, about forty in number, were accommodated in the barn with beds of soft hay and rugs.

The ease with which the ladies out here do without the paraphernalia, considered in England as necessary in preparing for a ball, struck me greatly at this, my first colonial one. The dressing of a young lady at home is a big affair, embracing an elaborate costume, an equally elaborate toilette, hair-dressing, and goodness knows what all, and concluding generally with an elaborate bill. Out here a light dress of muslin or some similar material, relieved with a little ribbon, and hair ornamented with a flower or two, constitutes the full evening costume of a young lady. She looks quite as nice as her semi-manufactured rival in England, and there is no prospect of a big bill for papa in the immediate future to mar her evening's amusement.

The gentlemen are equally negligent. If they have dress clothes, they put them on; but if they have not, they appear in whatever cut of black coat they happen to be the proprietors of, and enjoy themselves every bit as much as their swallow-tailed companions.

Before I left Mr. M——'s residence, he informed me that the fish-preserving scheme had turned out a failure, and that my bearded acquaintance had received a letter from his partner in the Waikato, in which he stated that the fish forwarded in the two tubs had sold readily at one shilling each, but had made all who partook of them very ill. "He presumed," he wrote, "that there must be something wrong with the German preserving preparation," and concluded by stating that as he had no wish to be apprehended for manslaughter, he must decline to have anything more to do with the business.

CHAPTER XV.

THE FORESTS OF NORTH NEW ZEALAND.

With the failure of the German preparation, my hopes of being made manager to the Fish Preserving Company vanished. I cannot say I had built much on it, so did not take the matter very deeply to heart. If the industry had been fairly started, the post of coroner in the Waikato might have been worth looking after. The ultimatum of the Waikato partner, however, nipped the business in the bud, and probably saved some lives.

No prospect of getting professional work had yet shown itself; and the only post I had succeeded in obtaining was that of correspondent to the Auckland weekly paper, an appointment of not a very lucrative nature.

Time, however, by no means hung heavily on my hands. There was plenty to do about my place, which had been much neglected. The weeds were disputing possession with the fruit trees, and had they been left undisturbed much longer I think would have gained the day. A peculiar kind of thistle, called the "cow thistle," grew everywhere luxuriantly, and docks with roots as thick as a man's arm were abundant.

I became familiarised with hoeing, digging, pruning fruit trees, and the use of the axe. The latter is a most necessary accomplishment in this part of the colony, as to the axe every one trusts for his supply of fuel. When I first attempted to wield it, each blow struck jarred my hands and arms tremendously, and at the same time made little impression on the wood; but at last I caught the trick, and am now a fairly good axeman.

Small tea-tree, or "Manuka," to use the native name, is principally used for firing. The wood is hard and close-grained, and gives out a great amount of heat. It grows in large and dense patches called "scrub." The trees in the scrub generally stand about a foot apart, run up straight for some twelve feet, and then break into a small bunch of branches. If tea-tree happens to be isolated, it becomes a spreading tree of fair dimensions, though it never grows sufficiently large to be employed much in carpentering. It is always more or less in flower

—a beautiful small white flower—with which at some seasons of the year it is completely covered. Not only is tea-tree universally used for firewood, but it supplies the material of which most of the fences up here are composed, and is preferred to any other wood for wheel-spokes. It is, therefore, one of the most useful natural productions of the colony.

North New Zealand boasts of a great variety of splendid timber, of which the Kauri pine (*Dammara australis*) takes the lead. These giants of the forest attain a girth sometimes of between forty and fifty feet, and grow up perfectly straight for sixty or seventy feet before throwing out branches. They reminded me when I first saw them of the toy trees with little round stands that used to be sold with boxes containing wooden animals. If the reader can imagine one of these toy trees magnified some six or seven hundred times, he will have a fair idea of what a Kauri looks like. Its foliage resembles somewhat that of the ornamental shrub known as the "Monkey plant," the leaves being stiff and glossy.

The Kauri is used more extensively than any other New Zealand wood for building purposes. It is a magnificent timber, and if properly seasoned, neither shrinks nor warps. Very few of the bush owners, however, can afford to let timber lie idle for any length of time, and therefore the majority of the Kauri used is not seasoned, and shrinks very much both ways. So much is this the case, and so unreliable is the timber considered through insufficient seasoning, that a clause has been inserted in the specification for the New Auckland Custom House, now about to be erected, which states that Baltic timber, and not Kauri, is to be used for sashes, architraves, mouldings, &c. As Kauri is very easily worked, and admits of a splendid polish, it is greatly to be regretted that with such timber in the province the architect should have deemed it necessary to specify Baltic timber. It is nevertheless true, however; and the cause may be summed up in six words, "High wages and want of capital," the great bane of New Zealand, felt not only in the timber trade, but in all other industries that have been established.

In getting out the Kauri, an immense and at times reckless destruction of young trees takes place, and for this reason the time is not far distant when the Kauri pine will be a tree of the past.

From an official report of Mr. T. Kirk, F.L.S., Chief Conservator of State Forests—for a copy of which I am indebted to the courtesy of Mr. S. P. Smith, Assistant Surveyor-General—it appears that the total extent of available Kauri forest now existing does not exceed two hundred thousand acres, and placing the average yield at the high rate of fifteen thousand superficial feet per acre, the Kauri at the present demand will be exhausted in twenty-six years. If, however, the demand increases in the same ratio as it has shown during the last ten years, it will be worked out in fifteen years. When we consider that the Kauri timber trade is one of the mainstays of the North Auckland district, this is a most alarming statement. The export trade amounted last year to the value of £136,000— more than five times as much as the timber trade of all the rest of the colony put together ; and it is difficult to see what is to take its place when the last Kauri has been felled. In Mr. Kirk's report no allowance is made for probable loss by bush fires, which in the dry weather are constantly breaking out, and which are generally ascribed, rightly or wrongly, to the carelessness of gumdiggers or to vindictiveness. Fires in the heavy Kauri bush last a long time when they once get hold, and do an immense amount of damage. There is a Kauri bush at the present time on fire in this riding of Matakohe which has been alight for the last five or six months. A large quantity of timber must be destroyed in this way, and the contingency of fire further lessons the probable duration of the Kauri forests of North New Zealand.

The task of felling and getting the timber out of the bushes is a difficult and dangerous one. The country north of Auckland, where Kauri abounds, is usually very broken, and seldom admits of a tramway being laid down to carry the logs on. When the timber is on high ground, the usual method adopted is to cut the logs into suitable lengths with cross-cut saws, move them by means of timber jacks and immense teams of bullocks to the brow of a convenient incline, and let them slide down a well-greased shoot composed of young Kauri trees, a great number of which are thus annually destroyed.

If the bush happens to be on the borders of the Kaipara, the logs are placed behind booms until enough are collected to make a raft. If, however, it is situated some little distance from deep water, the logs are laid in the bed of an adjacent creek, higher up in which a dam is formed and the water stored. When sufficient logs are collected, and sufficient water stored behind the dam, the sluices are opened, and the logs washed down to the Kaipara, where they are gathered, chained together, and towed to their destination.

Ordinary Kauri timber presents, when polished or varnished, a wavy appearance, and is darker in some places than in others; but occasionally Kauri is mottled, and when this is the case it is very valuable for veneering purposes, being worth from £3 to £5 per hundred superficial feet, while the average price of ordinary Kauri is only ten shillings per hundred feet.

The mottling is sometimes caused by the tree throwing out an excessive number of branchlets, and at others by a sort of disease in which the too rapid development of cellular tissue prevents the proper expansion of the bark, and small portions become enclosed in the sap wood, and form the dark mottlings. Mottled Kauri trees are usually found in rocky situations.

The total area covered by forest in the North Auckland provincial district—of which the Kaipara forms a part—is estimated by the chief surveyor to be seven million two hundred thousand acres, about one million six hundred and seven thousand acres being held by the Crown. One peculiar feature in these forests is that while they possess several trees—among others the Kauri—not to be met with in any other part of New Zealand, they still contain all the trees found elsewhere in the colony.

The Puriri (*Vitex littoralis*), sometimes called the New Zealand oak, is perhaps next in importance to the Kauri, on account of its great durability. It is principally used for railway sleepers, house blocks, framings of carriages, and fencing posts. It makes excellent furniture, and is said to equal the English oak in strength and durability. Sometimes the tree grows to a height of twenty feet in the trunk, and Puriri logs have been cut nine feet in diameter.

The Kahikatea (*Podocarpus dacrydioides*), a white pine, is a magnificent-looking tree, often reaching a total height of one hundred and fifty feet, with a barrel clear of branches seventy-five feet long. Its timber is highly valued for the inside lining of houses.

The Totara (*Podocarpus totara*) is employed in making wharf piles, telegraph posts, sleepers, and in the construction of houses and furniture. It occasionally grows to a height of seventy feet or so, perfectly straight, without a knot or branch, and is used by the natives for making canoes, some of which, seventy feet in length, have been hollowed out of Totara logs. It is the only wood that successfully withstands the ravages of the *Teredo navalis*.

The Pohutukawa (*Metrosideros tomentosa*) is a very handsome tree, usually to be found growing near the water's edge. At Christmas time it is covered with beautiful red blossoms, and on that account is called New Zealand holly. The trunk is very hard, and is invaluable for knees and timbers of ships and boats.

The Rata (*Metrosideros robusta*) has until lately been considered by most people to be altogether a parasite, but it has now been proved beyond doubt that its seed is deposited by birds, or the wind, in the fork of a tree, where it germinates and sends forth two or three roots which creep down the trunk to the ground. These roots, as they grow, press on the supporting tree, until they cause its death, and the Rata then stands alone. The wood is very hard, and when not too twisted, may be split into very good fencing rails.

The Rimu (*Dacrydium cupressinum*) is a very stately pine, with drooping branches like the weeping willow. It grows up straight for about sixty feet, with a slightly tapering barrel some two or three feet in diameter at the ground. The grain of this wood is red, streaked with black, and it makes splendid furniture, balustrades and railings for staircases, panels for doors, &c.

There are a great many other varieties of trees in the North Kaipara forests, which, however, I will content myself with stating are most of them exceedingly beautiful in grain, and should find places of honour in cabinet and furniture makers' work. In spite, however, of the beautiful woods at command, the furniture-making trade has made but little progress in Auckland, and I presume the high price of labour and want of capital prevent it from being pushed.

The bushman who fells the timber and rolls out the logs receives an average wage of thirty shillings a week, as well as his food, or, as it is called here, his "tucker;" the towing charges are high, and the railway rates from Helensville to Auckland exorbitant; and so by the time the timber has passed through the mills and left the furniture-maker's hands, the excessive payments for labour, railway and towing charges, have made the articles into which it has been converted so expensive, that the trade is killed.

The annual output of timber in the Auckland district is estimated at about one hundred million superficial feet, and the larger proportion is employed in the construction of houses, bridges, &c., in the colony.

Timber houses are a great deal more durable than many people would imagine : there are some still standing in Auckland—in fairly good condition—built nearly forty years ago. The mode of erection usually adopted is briefly as follows. Puriri blocks, sunk in the ground deep enough to insure a good foundation, and of sufficient length to project above the surface two or three feet, are set up in rows four or five feet apart. On these blocks—the tops of which are sawn off perfectly level with one another—is laid a frame of timber, marking out the rooms and passage, and on this the superstructure is raised. Instead of slates or tiles, thin strips of wood, called shingles, split off small blocks of Kauri, are most commonly used for the roofing, though corrugated iron sometimes takes their place. In the better class of house a brick chimney runs through the structure, but in the smaller and cheaper ones a wide wooden chimney is erected at one end.

CHAPTER XVI.

THE LABOURING-MAN SETTLER.

I TRUST the kind reader will excuse the somewhat sudden departure from my narrative to the forests of North New Zealand, which characterised the last chapter, and will now also pardon an equally abrupt return to my humble doings.

When in Auckland I had bought three or four books on colonial fruit culture, all of which I found, on investigating their contents, advocated thorough drainage. I therefore made up my mind to attempt to drain my smaller orchard, and in order to do so successfully, carefully took the levels, and planned out the drains. I tried digging them myself, but the work progressed so slowly, and my hands became so uncomfortably blistered, that I was obliged to call in extraneous aid, and applied to a labouring man, a settler in the district, for his assistance. His terms were seven shillings a day, which I with much reluctance agreed to give. He arrived at the scene of his labour at eight o'clock on the morning following my interview with him, took a full hour in the middle of the day for his dinner, and left off work at five P.M. with a punctuality worthy of a better cause. At the end of three days he had opened one drain to the required depth; it would take ten of them to drain the orchard, and they would require, in order to keep them open, filling up with tea-tree, the cutting and carrying of which would probably equal the cost of the digging. I therefore came to the conclusion that draining my orchard would go a good way towards draining my purse, and determined to abandon the project.

The labouring man, when I informed him of my resolution, said, with a melancholy air of superior wisdom, "I guessed you'd soon get tired of it," and appeared quite resigned to his dismissal.

Among the labouring-men settlers (by which expression I mean those who go out to work at so much a day) there is to be found a type of humanity quite distinct from any other I have ever met with. Specimens of this class are sometimes just sufficiently educated to be able to read and write, and sometimes have no education at all, but still they believe themselves—truly and earnestly believe themselves—to be gentlemen. They are to be distinguished by solemn-looking faces, to which beards are generally attached. They very seldom smile, never laugh, and always speak slowly and deliberately, often using long words in wrong places.

This variety of the labouring-man settler delights in being called by the prefix Mr. ——, and it would give him unspeakable joy to receive a letter addressed Mr. ——, Esq. Imported probably into New Zealand in its early days, he knows little more than the Maori about the doings of the great world. Yet he is very self-opinionated, and considers Auckland the finest city in the universe. He does a good deal of "gassing" in a solemn manner, which inclines a stranger to give credence to his romances, until their dimensions become too large to be swallowed. In spite of these little failings, he is steady, honest, and temperate, and his chief fault lies in his believing himself to be what he is not, and what he never can be. He is a square man continually trying to fit himself into a round hole, a task impossible for him to accomplish, while the effort to do so sours his disposition and renders him melancholy. He either possesses extreme religious views, and is very bigoted and narrow-minded, or he has no religion of any kind. Of course he owns land, given him by the Government that brought him out. He works fairly hard on his own property —harder, I am inclined to think, than he does when engaged on any one else's; and the fact of his being a landed proprietor, probably gives him the impression that he *must* be a gentleman, and is the cause of all his futile strivings and unhappiness.

I do not mean for one moment to assert that all the labouring-men settlers are like the above. There are many who have been soldiers, sailors, or have followed some occupation, before they settled in New Zealand, which has given them opportunities of seeing life. Their views are therefore larger and wider, and they have learnt how to laugh. Still, in most of the settlements I am acquainted with, are to be found some examples of the class of settler I have described.

Having abandoned the drainage scheme, I turned my attention to effecting other improvements, and amongst them built a small pier or wharf of limestone rock, at the sea end of which I kept my punt, and so could get away in it as soon as the tide came in, instead of having to push it over the rough limestone beach.

One day a young Matakohe settler called, and asked me if I would care to join a small party, to ride out on the following morning to the Wairoa swamp, to try and destroy a dangerous wild bull that was roaming about there, and which a few days previously had gored the speaker's horse, when he was cattle-hunting, he himself only escaping by jumping into a creek. He also told me there were great numbers of Pūkŏkŏ or swamp-hens there, and that after despatching the bull, we might be able to have some Pūkŏkŏ shooting. I at once agreed to join the party, and that night visions of roaring bulls with distended nostrils, lowered heads, and erected tails attended my slumbers.

I awoke next morning with a sort of Gordon Cumming feeling about me, and made preparation for my first day's big game shooting. Armed with a rifle and fowling-piece, I mounted my horse, and sallied forth to the place of rendezvous, where our party, four in number, had already assembled, and after a ride of about nine miles, we reached the edge of the swamp. Two of the party who had not brought guns, then proceeded on horseback, to discover the whereabouts of the game, and one of them dismounted to examine a clump of tea-tree, growing on a high mound about four hundred yards out on the swamp.

There the animal was, sure enough, and the rash disturber of his peace had only time to climb a friendly cabbage-tree when he charged.

We could see the man in the tree, but no sight of any animal, and wondered what he could be doing up there, until he shouted out that he was bailed up by the bull. Upon receiving this intelligence we sallied forth to endeavour to persuade the beast to raise the siege, and the mounted settler, by cracking the stock whip which he carried in the vicinity of the scrub, at last succeeded in getting the bull to come out on to the open swamp, when I immediately fired and put a rifle ball through his stomach. Another bullet from a fowling-piece brought him to the ground, and thus ended my first and only bull hunt—a very tame affair. If the animal had seen and charged us when we were on foot on the open swamp, before I handicapped him with a bullet, it would probably have been quite exciting enough for some of us, but as it turned out, the bull did not give half the sport the pious man's cow afforded, when her calf was taken away.

There are great numbers of wild cattle in the back country of this district, and I am told that most exciting adventures at times take place with them, though I cannot speak from experience.

The two settlers who had not brought their guns, skinned the carcass of the animal we had shot, and cut off some of the choicest pieces of its flesh; and while they were so employed, the rest of us went on the swamp to shoot Pūkĕkŏ, which were there in great numbers. Every minute or two, as we pushed our way through the tall Raupo grass, Pūkĕkŏ would rise about thirty yards ahead, and we had some very pretty shooting, and made a heavy bag. The Pūkĕkŏ belongs undoubtedly to the same family as the familiar moorhen of the old country. It is, however, much larger, and is a very handsome bird. The neck, breast, and body are bright blue, the wings black, and the underneath part of the tail white. It has a flat red sort of comb or crown on the top of the head, and red feet. Its flesh is very good to eat in the New Zealand autumn, but only at that time of year.

CHAPTER XVII.

KAIPARA FISH.

ALTHOUGH I had been defeated in my scheme of draining my orchards, I did not on that account give them up in despair, but endeavoured to improve the condition of each tree by lightly digging round it, and mulching it with the weeds I had taken off the land. They seemed all to be growing nicely, and the peaches the first season yielded a tremendous crop of most delicious fruit; so many indeed had we, that besides almost living on them ourselves, we fed the pigs with them. It was a great season everywhere in North New Zealand for peaches, but since then some sort of blight has universally attacked the older trees. The why or the wherefore of the disease remains a mystery, and the matter is greatly exercising the minds of the most eminent authorities in the colony. All sorts of theories have been put forward, but no satisfactory solution has been arrived at. One might almost fancy that some personage possessing mysterious power, and suffering from too free indulgence in the delicious fruit, had cursed them, as the Abbot in the Ingoldsby Legends cursed the Jackdaw of Rheims.

Other fruit-trees, both English and sub-tropical, grow and fruit remarkably well in the North Kaipara, in spite of the fact that not a single orchard anywhere is drained. If every advantage were given the trees, what would they not produce!

The climate is eminently suitable to fruit-tree culture, and the slopes of the undulating hills present everywhere opportunities for planting snugly sheltered orchards. Fruit-growing ought to become one of the standard industries of the district; but before that can happen, the railway charges must be lowered very considerably. The first apple season after I was settled in Matakohe, I sent a case of splendid apples down to Auckland to be sold, and the sale just covered the freight.

The excessive and prohibitive railway charges tend to stop all enterprise. The railways are supposed to have been constructed to open up the country, develop its resources, and induce settlement; but as they are at present managed, it would be absurd to think of starting any industry, in which they would have to play an important part as carriers. Cheap railway freights and fares would naturally have a tendency to enhance the value of the land in the country which came within their influence, bringing it as it were in closer contact with the centres of population, and it may therefore be inferred that owners of suburban estates—which must suffer by country properties being rendered more marketable—are by no means anxious for any alteration in the railway tariff, and suburban landowners are a power in the colony. The time must come, however, when in spite of all opposition, the freights will be lowered, and the sooner the better for the prosperity of New Zealand, and for the fruit-growing industry of the Kaipara. Enough, however, of railway mismanagement.

A settler who understood netting had made me a small fishing-net, and fish now formed a prominent feature at our table. Fishing wasted a good deal of time, however, as most of the fish are caught in narrow channels when the tide is running out, and the punt almost invariably was left high and dry, and had to remain until the tide flowed. I always in a day's fishing caught a great many more fish than we required for our own use, and it occurred to me to enclose a portion of the beach below high-water mark with a wall, so as to form a miniature fish-pond to keep the surplus fish in. As the tide flowed a self-acting valve let the water in, but prevented

My Fish Pond.

it from flowing out again when it ebbed. A lever connected with this valve, allowed me to empty the pond at pleasure.

The piscatorial residence—forty-six feet long, twenty-three feet wide, and five and a half feet deep—being ready for occupation, the next question to determine, was how to keep the fish alive after they were caught, until they could be transferred to the pond. To accomplish this, I made a sort of basket of wire-netting to hang over the side of the boat and keep the fish in, but it proved a failure, and I eventually purchased a little punt about six feet long, which had been built for a boy, but was too cranky to be used with any degree of safety. In this punt, fitted with a removable canvas cover, and filled with water, the captured fish were deposited, towed home, and transferred to the pond, where they soon appeared to be perfectly at home.

About this time I obtained the services of an able-bodied lad of some seventeen years, who understood farm work and a little carpentering. He used to fish for me at times, and caught so many fish that I tried sending fresh fish down to Auckland for sale there. The journey occupied, however, the greater part of two days, though the distance is under a hundred miles, and the fish did not arrive in town in good condition. If packed in ice, they would of course have kept perfectly fresh, as they were alive when sent from Matakohe; but I had no ice-making machine, and therefore was obliged to give the matter up.

I feel confident, however, that the fishery here only wants capital to develop it, to become one of the great industries of the North Kaipara. Its land-locked waters swarm with the finny tribe, and can be fished with impunity in any weather. Fish is by no means a cheap commodity in Auckland; but the population being small, the market there would soon be glutted. Sydney, Melbourne, and the other Australian ports, however, present a grand field for the disposal of the fisherman's spoils, and were fish sent away alive from here packed in ice, frozen by the Freezing Company in Auckland, and transported from there to Australia in ships provided with freezing chambers, I cannot help believing an immense trade would be done.

I have seen in the newspaper the price of fish called schnapper, quoted in the Sydney market at from thirty-six shillings to eighty-four shillings per dozen. These fish can be caught line-fishing in the Kaipara, at the rate of sixty or seventy an hour per line of two hooks, and of an average weight of about 9 lbs. each. The schnapper fisherman files the barbs off his hooks, that they may readily be extracted from the fishes' mouths; he also ties the bait securely on; and thus prepared, can haul the fish in as fast as he likes. The schnapper has most powerful teeth and jaws, and lives principally on cockles and

Sketch of Schnapper.

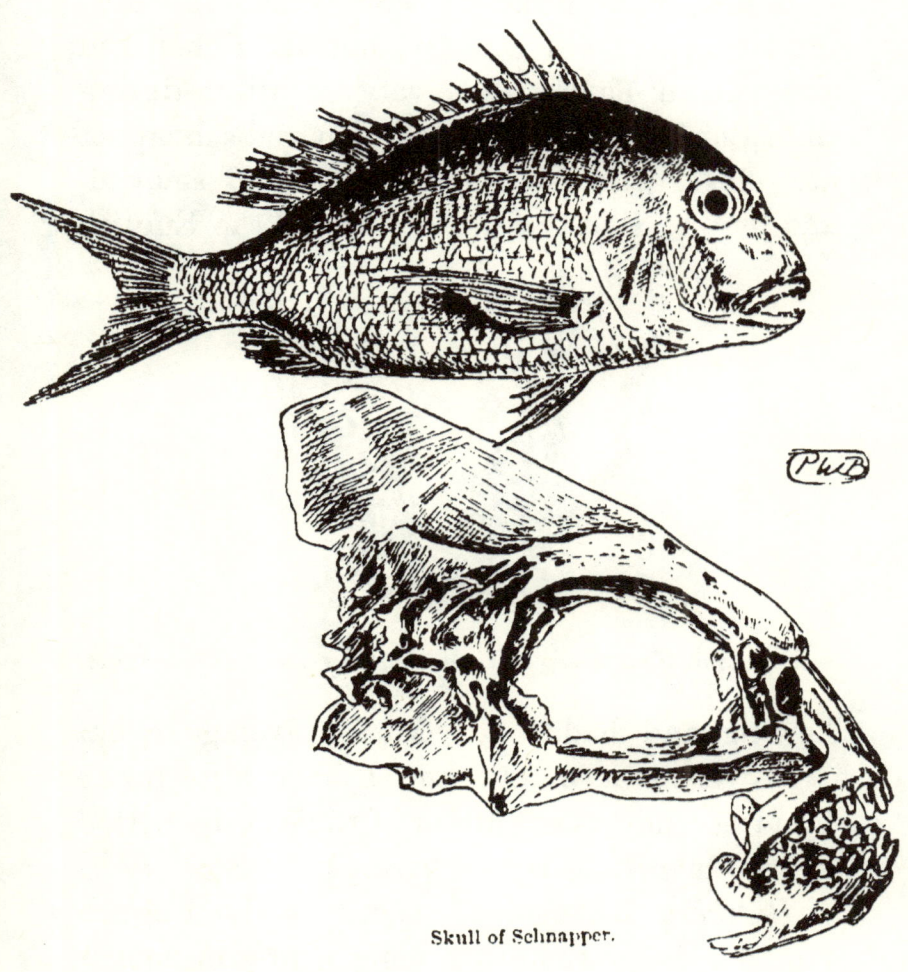

Skull of Schnapper.

mussels, the shells of which it crushes in its mouth without difficulty. It will, however, take almost any sort of bait, and is by no means a fastidious eater. The Kaipara waters swarm also with several other varieties of fish.

Mullet, resembling in appearance the grey mullet of the old country, but far richer and superior in flavour, are very plentiful during the summer months. These fish and schnapper are most delicious when salted and smoked, and may be said to fill the place of the English

Sketch of Lower Jaw of Schnapper, showing double row of teeth. (About half size.)

herring and haddock. Mullet average about 2 lbs. each in weight, and I have known one hundred and twenty dozen of them to be netted by two men in a day up here.

Patiki, a fish shaped exactly as the English flounder, but resembling more nearly in flavour the sole, are here in great numbers, and can be caught with a net in boat loads.

The *Kahawai*, weighing on the average 5 or 6 lbs., and modelled very much like the salmon, though finer in the tail, and with spotted sides. The resemblance unfortunately ends with the shape, for its flesh is dry and not over palatable. It lives principally on young mullet and Patiki.

The *yellow tail*, a sort of sea bream; a fish called locally the *king fish*, closely resembling in shape, fins, colour, and scales the fresh water tench; the *dog fish*, *eels*, and a small fish with a long snout called the *pipe fish*, complete the list, with the exception of the *shark*, and a fish called the *Stingarie*, doubtless a corruption of Stinging Ray. This fish—in form somewhat like the skate, with the exception that it has a long tail—attains a weight, at times, of about a quarter of a ton, and possesses a most formidable sting, armed with sharp-pointed barbs, and from six to eight inches in length, and about half an inch in width. This sting is situated at the root of the tail, and lies flat along it. When the fish makes an attack, it elevates its sting, and runs backwards with great speed at the object of its wrath. The Stingarie is of a discreet nature, however, and will never make an attack, unless driven to it. Its principal food, like the Kahawai, consists of mullet and Patiki.

Oysters and other bivalves, including Pipis (cockles) and escalops, also abound in the Kaipara. The rough corrugated shelled rock oyster, spoken of in my second chapter, are very abundant in places; and there is another kind, a smooth shelled oyster, very like the English native, which locates itself in deep water, and therefore is seldom met with.

Escalops, I think, must be plentiful, if one may judge by the number of escalop shells thrown up on the beaches near deep water. To procure these delicacies a dredge would be necessary, and dredges for shell fish are as yet unknown in the Kaipara, neither has the trawl net ever been tried, so it is impossible to say what unknown piscatorial treasures may yet lie hidden in the unexplored depths of the waters of our inland sea.

CHAPTER XVIII.

GODWIT SHOOTING.

WHATEVER accusations of remissness and lack of zeal and energy may be brought against the New Zealand Government, no one can assert with any degree of truth, that the surveys of this part of the country are neglected by them. Before one surveyor's pegs have had time to commence to decay, and the lines cut, become grown up with tea-tree scrub, a new survey is ordered, new pegs are put in, and lines fresh cut. I am told that the cost of these repeated surveys sometimes exceeds the value of the land surveyed, and without for a moment supposing that they are unnecessary or useless, one cannot help thinking that the money spent in resurveying outlying and comparatively uninhabited districts, would be more judiciously expended in making good roads in those places that are already settled.

There have been two surveys at Matakohe

over the same ground—or at any rate in a great measure over the same ground—during the four years I have lived there. One of the most efficient surveyors on the Government staff, Mr. J——, was with his party, at this time encamped on the outskirts of Matakohe, and he and his assistant, Mr. de C——, called on me, and an acquaintance sprang up which greatly helped to lessen the dulness of our country life.

Mr. J—— was fond of shooting, and whenever a day could be spared, we went out together with our guns. When I first became friendly with him—in April—pheasant shooting had not commenced, so we confined our attention to the wild fowl, the season for which had already opened, in consequence of the breeding time having been unusually early. The Acclimatisation Society has the power to alter the shooting season as it deems advisable, but the season for both native and imported game, usually extends from the 1st of May to the end of July. We enjoyed two or three good days' sport together, but the best I have ever had up here, was towards the end of April.

On this particular day, Mr. J—— rode in by appointment to have some godwit shooting, and as soon as the incoming tide reached my land-ing wharf, we embarked in my punt with our dogs, guns, luncheon, &c., in order to have some shooting before the flats became covered. I took with us one of my boys, a capital hand with the sculls, and his duty was to paddle the punt as quietly as possible, when we were coming up to birds, while my friend and myself placed ourselves as well as we could out of sight.

We first steered for a point about a quarter of a mile off, on which we could distinguish birds of some description. Mangrove grew in the shallow water off this point, and these I was careful to make use of, as a screen, as long as possible. As we neared the last one, I handed my boy the sculls, and crouched down in the stem, while Mr. J—— followed my example in the stern. Presently the last shelter was passed, and we came in full sight and range of a large flock of godwit. Up they rose to seek safety in flight, but the music of our guns rang out, feathers flew in all directions, and the dogs had their work cut out for some time. We dropped fifteen and a half brace with the three shots we got in; and when they were all bagged, we hoisted the sail, as a nice breeze was blowing, and shaped our course for a point called the

Tent Rock, where I knew godwit, red-shanked plover, and other birds loved to congregate.

When within about a quarter of a mile, the sail was lowered, my boy again took the sculls, and Mr. J—— and myself laid up in the punt. In spite, however, of all our precautions, we only secured there a brace of red-shanked plover, a black duck, and a couple of New Zealand sandpipers. We now sailed away with a leading breeze for an island lying about three miles distant, which is only covered at high water, adding a couple of duck and a brace and a half of red-shanked plover to our bag on the way. On the island we had some grand sport, as the tide was by this time over all the flats, and the birds did not like leaving the only feeding place remaining to them.

After bagging nine or ten brace of godwit and plover we turned for home, quite satisfied with our day's shooting, and anxious to fetch my place before the tide had receded from the beach. This we succeeded in doing, and had barely reached the house with our load of birds when rain began to fall, and was soon descending in torrents. As the next day was Sunday, and of course a day of rest for the surveyors, we easily persuaded Mr. J—— to sleep at our house.

All the evening and through the night the downpour continued, and on Sunday morning, when it was still raining hard, Mr. J—— told me he felt rather anxious about his men, as they were encamped close to a stream in a valley, with high hills on either side. His anxiety turned out to be well founded, for on that Saturday night, as Mr. de C——, the assistant-surveyor, and the three men were fast asleep, the stream overflowed its bank, and the water gradually rising at last washed their tents away, and they awoke to find the flood level with their beds, and a bitterly cold rain pelting down on them.

A surveyor's camp bed is constructed usually as follows :—

Four tea-tree stakes for legs are driven well in the ground, and cut off at a convenient height above it. A couple of sacks with holes cut in each corner of the bottom are then stretched on two six foot stakes passed through the holes, and these stakes are nailed securely on the top of those driven in the ground, thus forming the bed, on which is laid either dried ferns or Mongi-mongi as a mattress. The tents that were washed away were recovered uninjured, and beyond the loss of a tin pot or two, and the wetting of some boots and clothes, no great damage was done, as Mr. J—— had luckily planted his tent, containing the instruments, maps, &c., on high ground beyond the reach of flood.

Being flooded out, I am told, is by no means an uncommon occurrence in the lives of Zealand Government surveyors. Compelled to camp near running water, as of course they cannot spare the time to sink wells, and have no water tanks, sudden floods often overtake even the most wary. Indeed, being flooded out, working up to the knees in mud and water, swimming rivers, climbing almost impossible mountains, subsisting on the pith of the Nikan palm when provisions run out and cannot be renewed, rheumatic pains, fevers and agues, may be all said to fall within the usual experience of the New Zealand Government surveyor, and to become qualified to enjoy these experiences a special training is required, and a stiff examination has to be passed. There is no guarantee of the permanency of the appointment, and no retiring pensions are granted.

A young man may waste several of the best years of his life studying for the post of Government surveyor, which he may obtain only to be dispossessed of on the plea of retrenchment. The colony being so young, presents few openings for educated men to make a start in life. I sincerely trust, however, it will have something more promising to offer the rising generation when their time comes to go forth into the world.

CHAPTER XIX.

THE KAURI GUMDIGGER.

I AM going to commence this chapter by confessing that I find myself in a difficulty. All my endeavours to secure an appointment had proved abortive. I am anxious to stick to fact, and at the same time to interest my reader, but how can it be done, if I simply relate the details of my humdrum life as a country settler!

Three or four chapters back, I rushed off from my narrative into the New Zealand forests, and then apologised, but I can't keep perpetually apologising, and to prevent the reader from closing my book in disgust, I must ask him to hold me excused if I frequently bolt off the even course of my clodhoppery existence into subjects which are more interesting.

I have already briefly described one of North Auckland's greatest industries — the Kauri timber trade—an industry, alas! of destruction, and one whose days are numbered. There is another great industry which also owes its existence to the Kauri, both of the present and of bygone times. I mean the Kauri gum trade. This being the land of the glorious Kauri pine for all ages, of course forms the "Tom Tiddler's" ground of the happy-go-lucky gumdiggers, of whom there are at the present time over ten thousand in the North Auckland district. About £350,000 worth of Kauri gum was exported last year from the province of Auckland, principally to London and America. It is used largely in the manufacture of varnish and lacquers, and as there are no varnish manufactories of any importance in New Zealand, all the gum is sent away.

The three principal exports of the province of Auckland are Kauri gum, gold, and timber, and the export value of the former is greater than the combined values of the gold and timber. The gumdigger therefore plays a most important part in the province of Auckland, as without his assistance its export trade would look very shady, yet he is universally looked down upon by the sober-sided settler, who hardly ever has a good word for him. " He's only a gumdigger," is an expression I have commonly heard used, to imply that the individual indicated was a person of no importance.

The title "Gumdigger" itself may have something to do with the matter. It is not a nice word, and looks too much like "Gravedigger" at first sight. Possibly, too, the sedate settler may not think digging gum so intellectual and high-toned an employment as digging potatoes, fattening pigs, and the other duties which fall to his lot; again, the gumdigger proper is not a landowner; and yet again, he is often addicted to what he terms "going on the spree," and when he has changed his gum into money, to changing the money into strong waters. All these causes, I think, conspire together to lower him in the eyes of the extremely respectable, but ofttimes narrow-minded settler.

I have not the slightest wish to endeavour to defend the gumdigger for the intemperance and careless waste of money that too generally characterises him, but I will say, and say it without fear of contradiction, that he is exposed to far greater temptations than ever beset the settler. He lives an entirely isolated and a fearfully hard life out on the gum-field, and when he comes into a township, which he probably does every two or three months, and converts his gum into money, the temptation "to go on the spree" is great. He is unmarried, and has no particular use for the surplus money after his "tucker" bill is paid, and he spends it recklessly. There are savings-banks, it is true, but no one calls his attention to the fact that by depositing his surplus cash in them it will be making money for him while he is out on the gum-field, and the probability is that he does not know of their existence. The settler has a hundred improvements to make on his land, and has plenty of ways of employing his spare cash. Besides, he is generally surrounded by his family, and has not to endure the horrible isolation in which most of the gumdiggers' time is spent.

Not all gumdiggers, however, waste their substance. Many when they indulge in a holiday, enjoy themselves in a moderate and becoming manner. Not long since I was rowing by the Matakohe Wharf, and saw a stout, thick-set man, whom I knew to be a gumdigger, fishing off its seaward end. His legs were dangling over the edge, his back was resting against one of the mooring posts, in his mouth was a short clay, and by his side stood a bottle of beer and a tumbler. His face wore a look of placid contentment, and he was evidently enjoying himself thoroughly.

Gumdigging is exceptionally hard work, and

A Gumdigger's Holiday.

only a man accustomed to manual labour can hope to be successful at it. Some intelligence too and power of observation is required, in order that the digger may not waste time work-

THE KAURI GUMDIGGER.

ing in unlikely places. When an old Kauri tree dies and falls, its huge roots throw up a mound of earth, and the shape of these mounds indicate to an observing digger the direction in which the trees have fallen, although all signs of the trees themselves have entirely decayed away and disappeared, perhaps thousands of years ago. As the gum generally exudes freely from the Kauri, and collects in the forks where the trunk commences to throw out branches, by stepping sixty or seventy feet from the mound in the right direction, and digging there, gum will probably be found. The mounds themselves also offer good chances, and these are generally first attacked.

A gumdigger's outfit is not an expensive one. It consists of a spade, a gum spear, and a piece of sacking made into a bag and strapped on his back with pieces of flax.

The gum spear is a four-sided rod of steel, about four feet long, and pointed at one end. It looks very like a fencing foil, with a handle like a spade stuck in the end of it, instead of a hilt. If the field is a new one, or has been but little worked, this instrument is brought into use, and with it the gumdigger probes the ground in different directions, until he strikes a piece of gum, which, if at all experienced, he can tell at once from a stone, root, or other substance. He then digs it up, puts it in the bag, and recommences spearing. An old observing hand generally does a good deal less spearing than a new chum, but a good deal more putting in the bag. When a field has been dug over two or three times, as most of them have been now, the big lumps have nearly all been removed, and the method then adopted is to dig in the most likely places, on the chance of turning up gum with the earth. Here the observing digger again gets the pull, for instead of digging a patch right out as many do, he digs a spitful here and a spitful there, and generally manages to turn up gum.

My theory is, that by minutely examining the places where gum is turned up, and comparing it with the surrounding ground, the wide-awake ones have discovered something or other—I don't in the least know what—which indicates to them the most likely places to dig. Anyway, it is a fact that some gumdiggers earn their two and three pounds a week, while others working equally hard, if not harder, in the field, can scarcely pay their "tucker" bill.

After the gum has been dug up, it has to be

Group of Tree-Gummers under Kauri.

THE KAURI GUMDIGGER.

scraped, and this is generally done by the gum-digger before he offers it for sale. If an industrious man, his evenings are usually spent at this tedious work; and the more successful his day's digging, the more scraping lies before him in the evening, and it is considered a good

Gum Scraping.

ten hours' work to scrape a hundredweight of gum. When it is thoroughly scraped, it is easy to see the quality, and it is then sorted into boxes. The rarest kind is quite transparent and resembles lumps of glass; the next in order, is cloudy in places, yellowish looking, and very like amber, though much more brittle; some again is all cloudy, and the commonest sort of all is almost opaque. The clearer it is the higher its value, and the price for the first class, which is used in the manufacture of copal varnishes, ranges from about £70 to £80 a ton, according as the market is over or under stocked.

Very pretty ornaments can be cut with a pen-

Gum Scraper's Knife, constructed so that blade can be replaced when worn out.

knife out of Kauri gum, the surface of which may be afterwards easily polished by being rubbed with a piece of flannel soaked in kerosine oil. In most of the gumdiggers' huts (or whares, as they are called), and in settlers' houses in gumdigging districts, are to be found specimens of amateur gum-carving, among which, hearts are by far the most popular subject. I have seen flat hearts with sharp edges, rounded hearts, lob-sided hearts, elongated hearts, and many other varieties of Kauri gum hearts, which, though doubtless greatly admired by the personal friends of the carvers, could not be said to possess any commercial value. The material is too fragile for elaborate and artistic designs to be attempted, and no trade of any extent in Kauri gum carvings is pushed in the colony.

All the gum dug out of the gum-fields of course belonged to Kauri trees of bygone ages, and is sometimes called fossil gum. From the living Kauri, however, gum is constantly exuding, and forming in large lumps in the forks of the branches. To secure this it is necessary to climb the tree; but the barrel being of such huge dimensions, and rising like a pillar for sixty or seventy feet, it cannot be climbed in the ordinary manner. The plan generally adopted, therefore, is to tie a small weight to a long piece of strong twine or fishing-line, and throw the weight over the branches; the end of the thread held below is then slacked out until the weight is lowered within reach, when a rope is tied to the line, and hauled up over the branch and down again the other side. Climbing this rope, the gum-seeker gains a footing on the branch, and with a tomahawk, hacks out the gum and lets it fall to the ground. I have heard of another method of climbing by means of steps cut with a tomahawk in the barrel of a Kauri, but have never seen it done, and should think it an exceedingly dangerous operation. Climbing for gum in the ordinary way with a rope is dangerous work enough, and very often men meet their death when engaged in the occupation. Only a few weeks back the dead body of a native was found in the bush about four miles from here, lying at the foot of a Kauri, the rope dangling from a branch overhead, clearly indicating the manner of his death. Tree gum is not so valuable as the ordinary gum found in the ground, but it can be obtained in much larger lumps, and a good tree climber can make on the average between three and four pounds a week.

The Kauri gum industry cannot be considered as an unmixed blessing to the province of Auckland, inasmuch as it materially helps to keep up the price of labour. If a man cannot get the wages he wants, away he goes to the gum-fields, and although he probably only makes enough to just keep himself

Climbing Kauri for Gum.

THE KAURI GUMDIGGER.

alive, still he is his own master, and is always looking forward to doing better. The life he leads when gumdigging is a fearfully lonely one, and he would really be far happier and far better off, if he were working regularly for moderate wages at some factory, with mates around him, and a comfortable cottage to spend his evenings in, when his day's work is over.

The North New Zealand working-man cannot see this at present, however, and until he is forced to see it, the natural industries of the province of Auckland can never be developed.

Take, for instance, the varnish-making industry. Although New Zealand is the only country in the whole world which produces Kauri gum—one of the most important ingredients in varnish—yet it is all sent away in its crude state, for other countries to derive the benefits and profits consequent on its manufacture into varnish.

Before closing the chapter, I must say a word concerning the honesty of gumdiggers. Within a radius of twenty miles from here, there are several hundred men engaged in the occupation, and within that same radius we only possess two rural policemen. In spite of this feeble protection, however, I have never during my residence in the district, heard of a robbery being committed by a gumdigger, although many scarcely earn enough to keep themselves alive.

CHAPTER XX.

A STORY OF A BUSHRANGER.

We are indeed very seldom troubled in the North Kaipara district with thieves or burglars. No one ever thinks of bolting a door, nor do people hesitate to vacate their habitations for two or three days, leaving them entirely tenantless and unguarded. There are no wolves among us; we are all lambs (I was going to say sheep, but I won't).

This was the state of things, until a sort of amateur bushranger started business in the district, about eighteen months ago, and upset all our feelings of security. He was not a gumdigger, however, but a labourer employed by a gentleman sheep farming in Matakohe. As correspondent for the *Auckland Weekly News*, I sent the Editor the following account concerning his little enterprise :—

"A North Kaipara Bushranger.

"An individual has for some time past been wandering about the different settlements here, whose doings do not at all meet with the approval of the inhabitants. He has contracted an unpleasant habit of visiting houses at the witching hour of midnight, and extracting from the larders whatever comestibles he finds to his taste. His penchant for sweetmeats of all kinds is remarkable. He would risk his liberty for a bottle of lollies, while the sight of a jam tart would draw him through a plate-glass window. This gentleman rejoices in many names, Sullivan being the one he at present patronises. Last week he visited Paparoa and Maungaturoto, and regaled himself at several establishments. On Saturday he called at Mr. D.'s. store, Maungaturoto, the owner being engaged elsewhere. Sullivan, unwilling to disturb him, broke open the door, and captured a bottle of prime bulls'-eyes and some other articles. He next made a short stay at the Doctor's, but what he secured there I have not heard. Some time last week he honoured Mr. B. of Paparoa with a visit, took all the loose cash he could find, a jar full of sweet jelly, and a batch of bread, leaving a stale loaf in its place. Finding that creeping through windows, hiding in holes, and sleeping in the tea-tree scrub had had a very deteriorating effect on his clothes, he applied to Mr. H.'s store, Pahi, during the proprietor's absence, and selecting a suit to his satisfaction, left without a word. Last Sunday he was reported to have reached Matakohe, and probably his presence will be felt by some of the settlers before long. Naturally, his movements have excited, and still excite, a good deal of notice and criticism, and a few weeks back some settlers, taking an unfavourable view of his peculiar free-and-easy mode of existence, applied to a local constable to come and put a stop to his little game. In due course this functionary arrived, and a sigh of relief went through the several settlements—an arm of the law was with us, and confidence was restored.

"The energy displayed by this officer was indeed most reassuring. No sooner did he hear of a settler's house having been entered the previous night, than he was off at once to the place. No sooner did the news reach him of another depredation being committed elsewhere, than away he went again, and at last succeeded in capturing—not the man—but some mementoes of his travels. The story goes, that he very nearly captured the man himself, and would have done so, if the man, who is very powerfully built, had not unfortunately captured him instead. It was in this way. Having sighted his proposed captive, our energetic and plucky local official immediately gave chase, and was evidently gaining ground, when the pursued suddenly crouched down in some tea-tree scrub. 'Now I have him,' thought the exulting rural representative of the law, and in another instant he was on the back, and his hand was on the collar, of the larder-breaking Sullivan, while in a voice of thunder he shouted, 'I arrest you in the name of the law.' Had the midnight prowler any sense of decency and the fitness of things, now was the time to show it by resigning himself quietly to his fate and the majesty of the law. But no! the bump of reverence must indeed be wanting in the cranium of this sweet-toothed bushranger, for instead of thus comporting himself, he actually (so runs the tale) passed his hand over the constable's shoulder, grasped his coat collar, and raising himself from his stooping posture, marched off with the highly indignant officer kicking and struggling on his back. On arriving at a creek, he shot the representative of the law over his shoulder into the water like a sack of coals, and retired into the bush to suck lollipops. After this episode our rural official returned to his home (eighteen miles away) to consider what was best to be done, leaving word, however, at Paparoa that should the knight of the jam tarts and bulls'-eyes be seen anywhere, he was to be detained until our rural official could come over to arrest him. Mr. Sullivan has made his presence felt several times since, but there always seems to be a difficulty about inducing him to remain in any one place sufficiently long to call in the services of our rural officer. Another rural officer from the Wairoa has now come forward, and is at present at Maungaturoto, while Sullivan is here. By the time the rural officer arrives here, the wily Sullivan will probably be at Pahi. If he could only be induced to partake of some carefully doctored jam tart, I think the rural officer would be more evenly handicapped. As it is, unless our volatile visitor gets a sunstroke, or accidentally chokes himself with a bull's eye, I fear a good many more larders will be emptied and a good many more jam tarts reported missing before he is safely placed under lock and key in Mount Eden Jail."

This lollipop-sucking bushranger for several

weeks completely baffled all efforts to arrest him, and pursued with impunity his meteoric course, leaving behind him a well-defined train composed of jam tins, lolly bottles, pie dishes, infuriated settlers, and rural policemen. He was finally captured near Helensville, about sixty miles from here, and in due course brought before the magistrates at Pahi, who committed him for trial. I rode over to be present at the hearing of the case, and in returning after dark, my horse shied, the saddle, too loosely girthed, slipped round, and I was thrown, the result being concussion of the brain. An acquaintance, a Paparoa settler, got me home somehow or other, and for three days my mind was wandering, during which time my poor wife had to attend to me entirely unaided, as on the very day of my accident she had dismissed our servant girl for dishonesty. The principal storekeeper in Matakohe kindly came at once, offered his services, and telegraphed for the doctor, who unfortunately was engaged attending a serious case at a distance. When he did arrive he said my wife had done everything he could have done, and that I was going on all right. It was months, however, before I could get about again, and neither my wife nor myself are likely to easily forget the North Kaipara bushranger, now safely installed in Mount Eden Jail, and about half way through the term of three years' imprisonment with hard labour to which he was sentenced.

CHAPTER XXI.

SPORTS.

A GRAND opportunity for an energetic bushranger might be found on the Pahi regatta and sports day, generally held in January. Then every one, masters, mistresses, children, and servants turn out, and leave houses and their contents to look after themselves. It is one of the chief events we look forward to in our uneventful lives up here, and a most sociable and enjoyable day is always spent, for every one seems light-hearted and happy on a Pahi sports day. Luncheon parties are given on board cutters, owned by neighbouring settlers, and moored so as to command a good view of the races; picnic parties are held on the bright shelly beach, while the settlers who live in the township itself keep open house.

Our punt usually conveys us to the scene of gaiety, distant about four miles by water, though over twelve by land. It was on our first visit on a regatta day that I became acquainted with a singular colonial institution known by the name of "planting." My introduction came about in this way. I had not long disembarked my wife and children at the township, after a somewhat boisterous trip, when a gentleman whose acquaintance I had lately made came up, and after shaking hands with us all, whispered mysteriously in my ear that he had a plant near, and wished me to come with him. Having secured seats for my party, I followed, wondering what sort of plant it could possibly be that required mentioning in such strangely subdued tones. My conductor soon came to a clump of tea tree, where, stooping down, he commenced groping about among the undergrowth, and at last produced a bottle containing some liquid, which I shortly after discovered to be brandy and water. What a curious plant! and in what a curious position to find it! The tea tree (symbolical of blue ribbonism) protecting and sheltering the deadly brandy and water plant. Here is food for reflection indeed, but let it pass! There were plants (of the class alcoholic) in all directions that day, from the humble beer to the haughty three star brandy plant.

An hotel has since been opened in Pahi, and

there is now no necessity for planting, though the system—which will doubtless strike with horror some of my readers—is still in vogue in most country districts on the occasion of any public gathering. In common justice, I am bound to say that I saw no one on that day at Pahi the slightest degree the worse for the peculiar gardening operations; in fact, unless like a bee gathering honey from flower to flower, some thirsty soul had made a round of the plants, which he could only do on receiving a general invitation from the proprietors, they were harmless enough, and the system must be regarded simply as a method adopted by colonials to show good fellowship.

To return to the regatta. Three or four hundred persons were by this time assembled. My wife had joined, by invitation, a party of ladies—the wives of some of Mr. Hay's heroes in "Brighter Britain"—on board one of the moored yachts, and I leave her deeply engaged in that enjoyment so dear to most ladies—a good gossip—and stroll on to the wharf to see the cutter race started. After some little delay, and a good deal of shouting, the seven boats entered for the contest are in position, the gun is fired from the umpire's boat for the start, and they all become suddenly covered with canvas, and are off. It is blowing half a gale—but what care they. Up go their gaff topsails, and the boats careen over until you can almost see their keels. Most of them carry extra hands for ballast, and this live ballast hangs itself over the windward rail. Away they go, till they look like toy yachts in the distance. Now they round the buoy, and beat up for home. One boat misses stays and goes ashore, another carries away her topmast, and a third springs her bowsprit and gives in. But nobody seems to mind—every one appears happy—owners of the damaged crafts and all. On the wharf, which is crowded, a little mild betting goes on, and a gentleman (an old Etonian) gets up a shilling sweepstake in his hat. Bang goes the gun, as the first boat passes the winning post. Bang again, and the second boat is in. Then a voice whispers in my ear, "Come along, I've got a plant;" and I retire with the whisperer, and have a glass of ale.

While the cutter race is progressing a rowing match is started, and then a punt race is rowed, followed by another sailing race for open boats, a Maori race, and a model yacht race. After all the boat events have been run off, walking a greasy boom fixed out from the end of the wharf is indulged in; and after that the landsmen have a turn, and a move is made for the greensward, which reaches down to the beach. Here are erected hurdles for horse-jumping, in which several Maoris (who are great at sports) are competitors; next comes pole leaping, long jumping, foot races, &c.; and the sports conclude with an obstacle race, in which the competitors have to crawl through bottomless tubs, and overcome all sorts of carefully devised impediments to their passage. A concert and dance in the public hall conclude a most enjoyable day's amusement. At its conclusion, horses are saddled, boats and punts got ready, and the assembly melts away, leaving the pretty township of Pahi bathed in the glorious light of the full moon, which here and there shines brightly on the sapless remains of the now no longer regarded colonial alcoholic plants.

Another great break in our monotony up here is the Matakohe Annual Race Meeting, in connection with which I at present hold the position of Hon. Secretary and Treasurer. At our last meeting, held in March, about four hundred persons assembled on the racecourse, and a capital day's sport was enjoyed. We had a grand stand capable of seating three hundred, refreshment booths, saddling paddock, weighing room, a tent for the Secretary, and a Judge's box. The jockeys all rode in colours, and the scene was altogether a very brilliant and enlivening one. The following events were run off during the day :—

The Maiden Plate, over a mile and a half course. Nine horses started, and winner received seven pounds.

Settlers' Race Handicap. Two miles course. Six started, and winner received seven pounds.

Handicap Hurdle Race. Two miles course, with eight sets of three feet six inch hurdles. Four started, and winner received eight pounds ten shillings, and second horse one pound five shillings.

Hack Hurdles, over a mile and a half course and six flights of hurdles. Five started, and winner received five pounds.

Maori Race, over a mile and a half course. Only three horses started, and winner received five pounds.

Matakohe Cup Handicap. Two miles. Seven started. Winner received thirteen pounds ten shillings, and second horse one pound ten shillings.

A Trotting Race, Pony Race, and Consolation Handicap, the winners carrying off between them twelve pounds, completed the events of the day.

Order was sustained by half the police force in the whole district, consisting of one constable of portly dimensions, backed by an imposing uniform and a shako. The money for the prizes was supplied by the takings at the gates, the nomination and acceptance fees, and the subscriptions of the members of the Club. There was no betting beyond a few shilling sweepstakes got up in the old Etonian's hat. No drunkenness disturbed the harmony of the day, or the equanimity of our stalwart protector. Legitimate sport, and nothing else, called us together, and legitimate sport we enjoyed to our hearts' content.

I am confident that great good results from such gatherings as the two I have described—the Pahi Regatta and the Matakohe Races. In the former, several of the competing cutters and boats, and all the punts, are locally built, and wholesome rivalry is excited among the builders, tending to improve the class of boat turned out by them. In the case of the races, the tendency is to improve the breed of horses, and to study more closely the most important animal in the colony.

These social gatherings also do good in another way, by bringing about a general handshaking and wiping out for a time of the petty jealousies and the miserable little bickerings and quarrels that too often exist among a certain class in these little settlements. Among such people the slightest thing is sufficient to cause a break in friendship. If Jones does not vote the same way as Brown, smash goes their acquaintance; if Robinson afterwards asks the discarded Jones to spend the evening, he is cut dead by Brown immediately; and if Mrs. Robinson appears in chapel with a more gaudy bonnet than Mrs. Jones possesses, the demon jealousy is at once aroused, and a coolness takes place between the two families.

The most active agent, however, in producing discord among the settlers is the law relating to straying cattle. As it at present stands, no compensation can be obtained for damage done by straying cattle unless the land trespassed on is enclosed by what is termed "a legal fence," which must be of a certain height and of certain forms of construction. A summons may certainly be taken out for trespass, and the owner of the cattle fined one shilling per head, but to do this involves a great loss of time, and is very little satisfaction.

The result of this law is that the man who has good feed on his land has to erect fences unnecessarily strong for the restraint of his own cattle, in order to keep out his neighbour's wandering animals. It certainly causes cattle to be very cheap, but at the same time does great injury to the legitimate farmer, who will not take advantage of this miserable piece of legislation, and who keeps his paddocks in good grass, and his beasts in proper restraint. Many settlers systematically breed calves, which, when about three months old, they brand with their initials, and turn out on the roads to get their living as best they may, knowing that if they do break into a neighbour's paddock, the chances are that they can show he has not a legal fence.

Surely it would be more just if the law made it compulsory for a man to fence sufficiently to keep his own cattle in, and not oblige him to fence to keep other people's out. Suppose twelve men take up land near together, only one of whom owns cattle, while the others crop and grow fruit trees, does it not seem grossly unjust that, in order to place themselves in a position to obtain damages, the eleven should be obliged to erect legal fences round their properties to keep out the twelfth man's cattle? Yet this is the law as it stands at present in New Zealand, and any change in it would probably meet with a great amount of opposition. We pay dearly enough for our laws out here, however, and the motto of all law-makers should be *Fiat justitia ruat cœlum.*

CHAPTER XXII.

SYSTEM OF GOVERNMENT IN NEW ZEALAND.

At the end of my last chapter I remarked that we pay dearly enough for our laws out here, and I will now try and explain my reasons for so thinking. In my humble opinion, we are altogether over-governed, and that this is one of the reasons why so many of our enterprises turn out commercially unsuccessful, and also why we do not make our own varnish, our own furniture, and do not push many other industries, for the prosecution of which the colony possesses exceptional advantages. We seem to be playing at being a big nation—a second Great Britain in fact—while our entire population does not reach the population of one of England's first-class towns.

Besides His Excellency the Governor, we have a Premier, styled an "Honourable," with a salary of £1750 a year, a ministerial residence, travelling and other allowances; six Cabinet ministers holding portfolios, receiving each a salary of £1250 a year, a ministerial residence, travelling and other allowances, and each styled an Honourable; one minister without portfolio, receiving a salary of £800 a year; a host of clerks belonging to the different ministerial departments, with salaries from £800 a year downwards; an attorney-general, solicitor-general, and several law officers; a Legislative Council, consisting at present, I believe, of a Speaker, a Chairman of Committee, Clerk to the Council, and forty-six members—each member being appointed *for life*, and receiving 200 guineas every Parliamentary session, a free pass on the railways, and the title "Hon." tacked on before his name.*

Then we have the House of Representatives, consisting of a Speaker, Chairman of Committees, Clerk of Committees, Clerk of the House, Sergeant-at-arms, Clerk of Writs, and ninety members. The M.H.R.'s are elected for three years, and each receives an honorarium of 200 guineas a session, a free pass on the railways, and has M.H.R. tacked on after his name.

* The Legislative Council is supposed to correspond with the House of Lords at home, but is called out here by the irreverent, the Old Man's Refuge.

It is doubtless a very proud and pleasant thing to be able to say we have a House of Lords, a Sergeant-at-arms, and all that sort of thing, but we are paying too dearly for the gratification.

In England, with an army and navy to support, and a National Debt of about seven hundred millions, the general government costs rather under fifty shillings per head. Out here, with a public debt of thirty-two millions, it costs double, though all we possess in the way of army and navy consists of one general, a few volunteers, and a small steamboat called the *Hinamoe* (*i.e.*, the sleepy), which, I believe, looks after the lighthouses, and carries the " Hons." and the " M.H.R.'s " about when they require change of air.

With regard to New Zealand's debt, it may be remarked that the money borrowed has not been thrown away on profitless wars, as is often the case with Government loans,—and that although I fear a good deal of money has been wasted, still there is something better to show than soldier's graves and tattered standards. There are telegraph lines, harbours, lighthouses, and about sixteen hundred and twenty miles of railway, which return at present a net profit of nearly three per cent. on their entire cost—over twelve and a half millions—and would probably return considerably more were the charges reduced so that farmers, orchardists, and others could profitably utilise them as carriers. Last year over four millions were expended in governing the colony, of which about one million was derived from the gross revenue of the railways, and three millions squeezed somehow or other out of the colonists. About half this sum of three millions went to pay interest on the public debt, and half the cost of government. It is with the latter item that our chance of retrenchment at present lies.

The population of the colony last year numbered about 620,000, comprised, as nearly as I can ascertain, of 120,000 unmarried men, women, widows, and widowers, 100,000 married men, 100,000 married women, and 300,000 children. It is clear that the 120,000 unmarried, and the 100,000 married men, have between them to pay, directly and indirectly, the whole sum necessary for the interest on the loans and the cost of government. The married man, with wife and average allowance of three children, has of course to contribute a very much larger share than the single individual, who has only himself or herself to support, and I will assume that the married man pays three quarters, and the unmarried one quarter. The former has therefore (without counting local rates) to contribute about £22, 10s. annually, half of which sum goes to sustain our expensive game of pretending to be a big nation.

How can labour be cheap when the above is the case! If the cost of government were reduced to one half, the married labouring man (and it is he that fixes the rate of wages) could afford to work for appreciably less than he now can, the cost of working the railways would be diminished, and the revenue from them proportionately increased. A sensible reduction in the price of labour would doubtless also most beneficially affect the commercial prospects of the colony, and probably cause the successful development of its many suitable industries.

Mr. Froude, in his book "Oceana," talks about the possibility of New Zealand repudiating her debt, and I trust he will not be angry if I say that the information given him on this point is about as accurate as the information he received concerning Kauri gum, to the effect that it was valuable because it made pretty ornaments. There is little fear of New Zealand repudiating her debt—as I think the figures I have given show—but I trust before long she will repudiate all the unnecessary paraphernalia of government that is weighing her down.

The colony may at present, I think, be likened to a goodly fruit tree full of bud and promise, but suffering from the ravages of a host of caterpillars, which are destroying its blossoms, and with them the chance of fruit.

A new Government pledged to retrenchment has lately been formed, and I trust the promises made on the platform will be fulfilled later on in Parliament.

Since writing the above, the following paragraph *referring to the late ministry* appeared among the items of Parliamentary news in the *Auckland Evening Star* of December 6, 1887.

"MINISTERIAL RESIDENCES.

"The following rather questionable items appear in the return of expenditure during the last six months on ministerial residences, and have created some comment:—

"Tinakori Road House (Sir J. Vogel's) : Overhauling lift, £11, 16s. 8d. ; gas-fittings for theatrical stages, £2, 9s. 11d. ; hire of piano, tuning and repairing, £10, 4s. ; 12 dining-room chairs, at 60s., £36 ; pink and gold breakfast set, £3 ; one spring lounge, £10 ; hire of piano, £7, 10s.

"Molesworth Street (Hon. E. Richardson's) : Re-covering suite in plush, £35 ; knife-cleaning machine, £4, 10s. ;

hire of piano, £8, 0s. 6d.; hire of piano repairing, £3, 5s.; three gas fires, £9; one dinner service, £14, 18s.; garden hose and fitting, £4, 1s. 4d.

"Tinakori Road (east) (Hon. J. A. Tole's): One walnut card table, £5; two spirit seltzogenes, £5, 2s. 6d.; flower-pots, £1; set best hangings, £9; one mangle, £8, 10s.; three pairs curtains, £5, 12s. 6d.; one child's bath, £1; packing piano from Christchurch to Wellington, £1, 10s.; freight, 9s. 8d."

CHAPTER XXIII.

KAIPARA INSECTS.

This part of New Zealand, as well as suffering in common with the rest of the colony from the ravages of the political caterpillar, is a good deal troubled with other insects, and an entomologist would find in the Kaipara rare

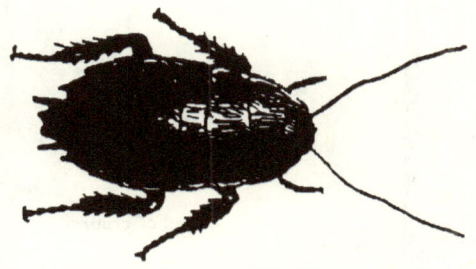

The Kauri Bug (life size).

opportunities of prosecuting his studies. Some of the specimens are so strange that they cannot fail to strike with their peculiarities the most unobserving, and I will venture to describe two or three of them.

The Kauri bug (called by the Maoris the

Kekereru), with its power of emitting a terrible and unbearable smell when alarmed, has been so often and so fully dealt with by writers, that I shall content myself with simply making a

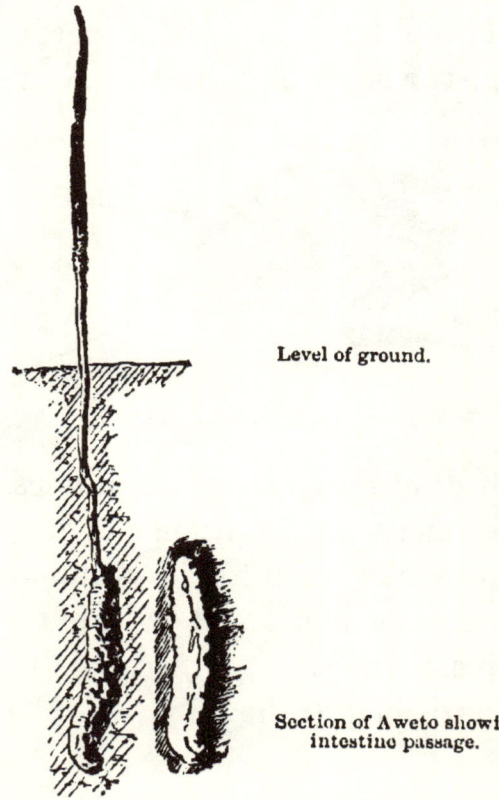

Aweto or Bulrush Caterpillar (two-thirds life size).

sketch of the insect, leaving its smell to the imagination of my readers, and will proceed to describe the most curious of the New Zealand native insects I have seen, called the bulrush caterpillar (*Sphæria Robertsia*)—native name, Aweto. This caterpillar becomes changed into a white vegetable substance while still retaining its caterpillar shape. It is from three to three and a half inches in length, and when about to assume the chrysalis form buries itself in the ground, and it is supposed that in doing so, some of the minute seeds of a fungus become inserted between the scales of its neck; these the insect, being in a sickly condition, is unable to rid itself of, and they vegetate and spread through the whole of the body, completely filling and changing it entirely into a vegetable substance, though retaining exactly the caterpillar form, even to the legs, head, mandibles, and claws. From the nape of the neck shoots one single stem, which grows to a height of eight or ten inches, its apex resembling very closely the club-headed bulrush in miniature. This insect plant is generally found growing at the root of the Rata tree. It has no leaves, and if the stem by chance becomes broken off, another arises in its place, though two stems are never found growing simultaneously from one caterpillar. When fresh, the vegetable substance of which it is composed is soft, and has a strong nutty flavour, and the natives are fond of eating it; they also use it burnt and ground to powder as colouring matter for tattooing purposes. In every instance the caterpillar is found perfect in shape and size, without any sign of contraction or decomposition, and it is therefore presumed that the vegetating process takes place during the insect's life. A section of the insect vegetable shows distinctly the intestine passage.

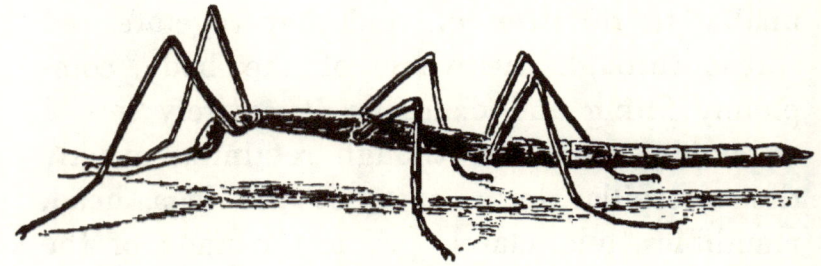

The Mantis (life size).

Another curious insect found here is the "Mantis," commonly called, on account of its shape, "the ridge-pole rafter." This insect has the power of changing its colour like the chameleon. It favours tea-tree more than any other plant, and if resting on a withered portion, assumes a corresponding brown colour, though when found on the young leaves it is a bright green. Its shape is most peculiar, and very suggestive of the name given it.

Another insect very commonly found in soft wood tree is called by the natives the "Weta," but by vulgar little boys "The Jimmy Nipper."

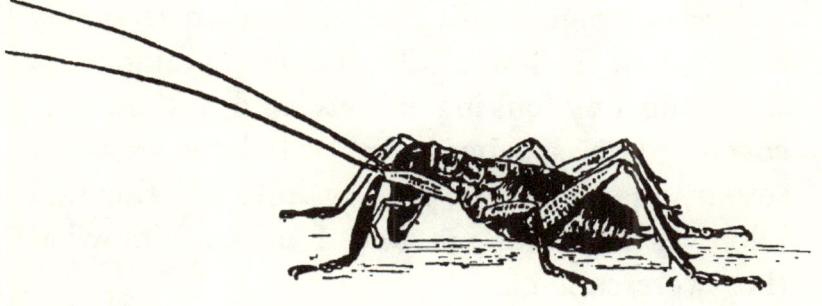

The Weta, Male (two-thirds life size).

It is a most repulsive and formidable-looking insect, with a body sometimes two and a half

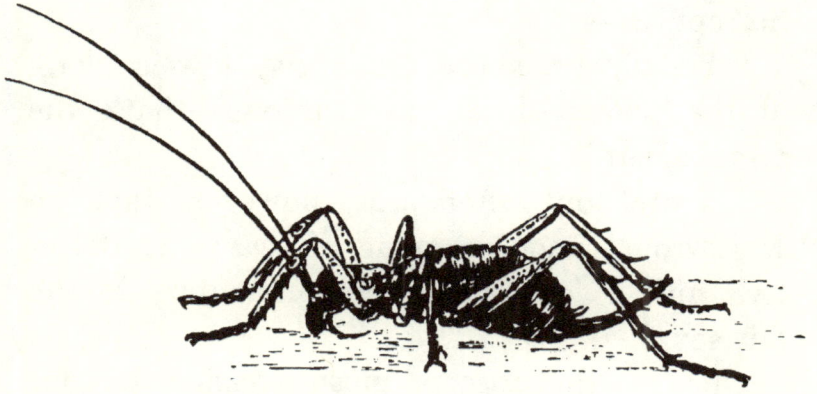

The Weta, Female (two-thirds life size).

inches long, and is capable of biting hard enough to make blood flow freely. The male and female differ considerably in shape, the male being provided with an immense pair of jaws. They have no wings, and their bodies are covered with a kind of horny shell.

I was engaged felling some dead trees in my bush when I first made the acquaintance of these uncanny looking insects, and I then discovered two specimens in a hollow tree. A settler, an old soldier, hailing from the Emerald Isle, was assisting me, and I asked him what they were called.

"Jimmy Nippers to be shure, sur!" he responded; "and by the same token, one's a male, and t'other's a faimale."

I inquired if he knew which was which, and he replied—

"Bedad, sur, shure that's aisy to see; look at the power of jaw in that one—that's the faimale, sur."

I found out afterwards, however, that he was wrong, and his mode of reasoning defective, and, I fear, hardly complimentary to the fair sex.

One of the insects most dreaded by our orchardists is an insect called the "Leech," about a third of an inch long, and very like a small slug. It sometimes attacks plum and pear trees in thousands, and completely denudes them of leaves. Shaking wood ashes over the trees is a very effective method of getting rid of these pests.

During some summers a kind of cricket also appears in immense numbers and eats the grass, and the bark off the fruit trees. The best remedy for these is to keep poultry, which relish them immensely, though the crickets in no sense return the compliment, as they give the flesh of the fowls a disagreeable bitter taste, and render them for the time unfit for the table. The eggs are not affected, however, and corn is saved, which is one point gained. Where crickets are undisturbed, they destroy all the grass in their neighbourhood, and then turn cannibals and eat one another.

We have not, I am happy to say, the dreaded Codlin moth up here, although it exists, I believe, in some parts of New Zealand.

Another destructive insect is a little brown beetle, shaped exactly as the lady bird. This insect confines its attention to the stalk end of the apple, round which it nibbles, until the apple withers and drops off. Last year the orchards in the neighbourhood were free from this pest, and I hope they have either moved to pastures new, or have been exterminated by some of our insect-eating birds.

The spider tribe is very fully represented, some specimens being of enormous size. One kind is said to be so dangerous that a bite from it endangers life. I have never, however, heard of any one in the Kaipara having been bitten.

One other insect, called the Mason bee, I must mention. This fly builds a nest of a kind of white mortar, stocks it with small spiders, and lives in solitary state. It lays its eggs in the nest, and the stored spiders, which are not dead, but appear to have been rendered insensible, are for the consumption of its offspring when they hatch out. The Mason bee has a very venomous sting, and is altogether an undesirable visitor, as it builds its habitation in all sorts of untoward places, sometimes even in the locks of doors.

We have numerous other kinds of insects, including a small sort of mosquito, a vicious little biting fly called the sandfly, and a locust, which, though differing altogether in shape from the ordinary locust of the East of Europe, makes exactly the same noise when settled on a tree.

My readers will probably think, from the foregoing alarming list, that we are an insect-ridden district altogether, but nature has provided us with plenty of help to keep down our pests. We have a beautiful little bird called the Blight bird, as small as some humming birds, which lives principally on flies and insects, though rather partial at times to grapes and figs; we have a bright brown vulture hocked bird —about the size of a lark, barred with brown and white on the breast, and with a beautiful metallic lustre on its feathers—which comes in flocks, and destroys great quantities of the Leech; and we have the imported Chinese Pheasant, which helps us greatly in the matter of slugs and crickets, though sadly given to rooting up crops of maize and potatoes, in consequence of which unfortunate habit it is looked upon as a deadly enemy by most of the farmers.

I asked my Hibernian naturalist friend one day how his potatoes were getting on. "Bedad, sur," he replied, "Oi niver had a crop come up so quickly; sure Oi'd only planted thim one day, and ivery mother's son of thim was up the next!"

His field, he afterwards explained, had received a visit from the pheasants in force.

In spite, however, of all the wrong-doing laid at the pheasant's door, I cannot help thinking it does a great deal more good than harm by keeping down slugs, crickets, and other destructive insects. I took 126 slugs out of the crop of one pheasant, and I have shot many others quite as well supplied. They also give us many a day's pleasure, and help to keep the larder stocked. With a couple of good dogs and a "white man" (as a good fellow is called out here) for a companion, what more enjoyable than a day after the long tails. You have to do a good deal of tramping for your sport certainly, and you don't generally make a big bag, but you never come home empty handed, and feel when your day is over that you have thoroughly earned the three or four—or perhaps five or six—brace of birds that are hanging up in your safe.

Heavier bags than these are often made, though it has not fallen to my lot to make them. Last season a young fellow here grassed fourteen and a half brace between sunrise and midday, and bigger bags than that are even sometimes recorded, but they involve to my thinking too great an expenditure of labour in the way of walking for pleasure. .

The full grown cock pheasant in New Zealand weighs from three to three and a half pounds, and the hen from two to two and three-quarter pounds.

There is one kind of shooting (native pigeon shooting) that may be indulged in, without any walking beyond that necessary to reach the shooting ground. All you have to do is to seat yourself in the bush under a clump of Taraire trees when the berries they bear are ripe, and wait for the pigeons to come and feed on them. As soon as the birds are settled on the trees, and are busy with the berries, you can blaze away as hard as you like, for they won't fly away or move until you bring them down. It is unadulterated pot-shooting, and there is not a single iota of sport to be got out of it with powder and shot, though with a rook rifle there might be some little fun. The Maoris, who are, as a rule, bad shots, are very fond of pigeon shooting—they being about the only birds they can hit—and I have seen them returning after a day's shooting with two or three horse loads of pigeons. The New Zealand bird, although looking larger than the English wood quest, rarely exceeds a pound and a half in weight.

CHAPTER XXIV.

A MAORI WEDDING.

BAD shots as the Maoris are generally considered, they are nevertheless very fond of sport, and are great fellows at horse leaping, running matches, and athletic amusements of all kinds. They are a fine, intelligent race of people, with plenty of fun and spirit in them, and are justly renowned for their hospitality.

About two years ago, the marriage of a daughter of one of the chief men belonging to a native village a few miles off took place; and I, in common with all the settlers in the neighbourhood, received an invitation to be present at the ceremony, and to partake afterwards of the wedding breakfast. My wife told me it would be the right thing to take some little bridal gift, and gave me a fan to present which had a good deal of gold and colour about it. I wrapped it carefully in some nice tissue paper, and thus accredited, rode off to the festive gathering. During the journey, the paper in which the fan was enveloped unfortunately became torn, and finally disappeared, and conceiving the impression that a horseman in knee breeches, spurs, and fan looked somewhat ridiculous, I was anxious to get rid of my present as soon as possible. On drawing near to the village, therefore, great was my delight to perceive the bride's father stationed at the entrance to receive his guests as they arrived, and I at once made up my mind to hand the fan over to him, but to my disappointment found his knowledge of English was as limited as mine of Maori, which consisted of one word, "Kapai," meaning, It is good.

I endeavoured to illustrate the action of the fan, and held it towards him, saying at the same time, "Kapai." He evidently viewed it with distrust, and appeared to think it something unholy, or a disguised infernal machine. Whenever I held it near him he backed, and every time I opened it he jumped. The more I cried "Kapai," the more he shied, and we were gradually working our way into the village, my host backing at every movement of the fan, and I leading my horse with one hand, and with the other manipulating the wretched bridal gift.

At last, just as I had made up my mind to pitch it away, a Matakohe settler came up who could speak Maori, and who soon altered the aspect of affairs. The fan was accepted most graciously, and was taken the round of the

He evidently viewed it with distrust.

Maori belles, each one of whom, when its action was explained, had a trial of it.

This helped to fill up the time, until our Church of England clergyman—who was to perform the ceremony—arrived, and we all repaired to a structure erected by the Maoris for the occasion, and made of Nikan palm leaves plaited together. The inside was very tastefully decorated with ferns and cabbage palms, and really did great credit to their artistic taste.

An "Ancient and Modern" hymn, in which the natives heartily joined, having been sung, the ceremony was performed in Maori, and a second hymn closed the service.

The bride and bridegroom then led the way to another construction of Nikan leaves, where the wedding breakfast was prepared. The happy couple took the head of the table, and the "Pakehas" (*i.e.*, the white men, literally "strangers"), were invited to first sit down, the Maoris waiting on them. The feast was ample, and consisted of wild pig, beef, vegetables, and plum pudding. When the Pakeha visitors had eaten their fill of the good things, the Maoris had their innings, and then the health of the bride and bridegroom, who still retained their position at the head of the table, was drunk in Gilbey's Castle A Claret, the toast being proposed by our local J.P., and translated by an interpreter to the Maoris. The bride's father returned thanks, and every one present shook hands with the loving pair and retired.

Some horse-jumping competitions among the natives brought the afternoon to a close, and I returned home very pleased with my day with the Maoris.

Giving place to their Pakeha guests, and seeing them duly satisfied before partaking of anything themselves, struck me as showing a very keen sense of true hospitality and politeness. They have also, I believe, a true appreciation of justice—at least I have often heard so, and in the only case which has come under my personal observation, the Maori concerned showed it in a marked degree. It occurred in connection with the race for horses owned by Maoris, run at our last meeting. The jockey of the leading horse—an Englishman—in coming up the straight for the post, deliberately pulled right across the second horse, thereby nearly causing an accident. A protest was entered by the owner of the second horse, and the evidence having been heard by the committee, it was unanimously decided to disqualify the leading horse, the second was declared winner, and the jockey censured. The leading horse could easily have won, and much sympathy was felt for its owner, who had lost the race through the bedevilment of his jockey.

When I handed the money to the Maori whose horse was pronounced the winner, I explained to him, through an interpreter, that he had won it simply through the misbehaviour of the leading jockey, and expressed my opinion that it would be fair to divide the sum with the Maori who had been so badly treated. He seemed to see the justice of the case at once, and without the least hesitation paid over half the money.

Civilisation has done, and is doing, great things for the Maoris. Among others it has taught many to drink, to swear in English, and to wear English slop clothes, which are quite unsuited to them and their habits, and to the use of which, many medical men attribute the pulmonary complaints so rife in their midst. They are constantly wading through streams, and getting wet through by rain, and they let their clothes dry on them (as they were accustomed to do when their skin formed the principal part of their garb), and thus sow the germs of disease, and hasten the inevitable day when the Maori will have been improved off the face of the earth.

No cannibalism exists, I believe, among them at the present time, though there are natives living who have indulged in it, and smack their lips at the thought. They say white men are too salt to be much good for the table, though young Pakeha children they pronounce to be "Kapai."

CHAPTER XXV.

SYSTEM OF EDUCATION IN NEW ZEALAND.

I MUST not lay down my pen without saying something about the New Zealand educational system, one of the best features in our colonial government, though possessing undoubtedly its faults.

The educational course is divided into three grades, viz., the elementary or public schools, the secondary or high schools, and finally the university. For the two latter, fees have to be paid, unless the scholar is clever and lucky enough to obtain a scholarship, in which case he or she can go through the whole course without any expense to the parents.

In regard to securing a scholarship, however, besides ability being necessary on the part of the pupil, a good deal depends on the capability of the teacher at the elementary school. This is an uncertain element, and constitutes, to my thinking, a flaw in the educational system.

Teachers at the elementary schools are supposed to pass examinations, and receive certificates of competency, but in the small up-country districts, teachers are often placed in charge who are not certificated, but are what are termed probationers. It is true that in each school-district, a committee is elected by the inhabitants, whose duty it is to attend to matters connected with the school and the teacher, and to report all irregularities to the head school board in Auckland. Very often, however, the members of these committees are uneducated men, sometimes even being unable to read or write, and it may be imagined that they are not held in much awe by the teacher, who does in such cases pretty well as he or she likes. Also, as the salary of the teacher is regulated by the average number of children attending the school, a good competent man naturally objects to a small district, and the consequence is, that the children in the country are not so well educated as the children in large towns.

This is a serious flaw in the working of the education scheme, but it is one that might possibly be overcome by the institution of Government boarding-houses in towns like

Auckland, where the children of country people who cannot afford to pay for private tuition, but who wish their little ones to be as well educated as possible, might be lodged at cost price by the Government. Another flaw, to my mind, in the system, is not allowing the Bible to be read in the schools, the result being that many children are allowed to grow up without any knowledge of their God or their Saviour, their parents naturally inferring that if it is considered unnecessary and unwise to teach Bible truths in the schools, there can be no necessity to teach them at home, even if they are able to, which in many cases they are not. Freethought and Deism has taken strong root in the province of Auckland, and I think the cause may probably be traced to the expulsion of the Bible from the New Zealand Government schools.

To counteract the evil effects of this blot in our educational system, we have our Church of England parsons, our Roman Catholic priests, and Wesleyan and Dissenting ministers of various denominations. In this district we are very fortunate in our Church of England parson, who is not only a gentleman, but is a conscientious and energetic man, as well as an agreeable and amusing companion. He has an immense deal of riding to get through, as his district is a very extensive one, containing about 800 square miles, and in the winter, when some of the roads are knee-deep in mud, his experiences must be at times terrible. He wears the orthodox dog collar, a clerical cut coat, riding trousers, and top-boots with the tops off, and thus accoutred, he travels about regardless of the weather, and unremitting in his endeavour to counteract evil, in whatever shape or form he meets it. He does not always spare himself time even to get his hair cut properly, for not long ago I saw him seated on a gentleman's verandah with a sack over his shoulders, while his friend, the owner of the house, was shearing him with a pair of sheep shears.

While we are thus happily provided with regard to our souls, our bodily welfare is not neglected, and our local doctor—a genial son of Erin, and a great favourite on all sides—rivals the parson in tending to our wants connected with his department. He also has an immense amount of riding to do, and is as much at home in the pigskin as some men are in their easy chairs. A forty-mile ride to see a patient he regards as a little holiday, and pulls up smiling at the finish. He is married, and in that respect scores against our parson. He is fond of sport, keeps his own hacks, a couple of racers, his double-barrelled central fire, and a brace of setters. He sings a good song (hunting ones are his favourites), is clever at his profession and attentive to his patients, and, in short, is what is known as a good all round man. I think I am therefore entitled to say that the North Kaipara settler, both body and soul, is in good hands.

The parson and the doctor are the two busiest professional men in this part of the world, although the doctor's practice is principally confined to accidents and additions to families. The Auckland lawyers perhaps have a fairish share of work at times, in connection with North Kaiparians, but engineers, to use a colonialism, have not a "show" at all—particularly now that the borrowing policy has been partially given up.

CHAPTER XXVI.

A MEETING OF THE COUNTY COUNCIL.

ABOUT a year ago the Government decided to create a new county, which was to be formed of the riding in which I reside, together with seven others. With this object eight councillors were elected for the eight different ridings. A meeting of these gentlemen took place to carry out the intentions of the Government, and to appoint certain officers. This was the first meeting of the Council, and I rode over in order to be present.

A large hall—at one end of which was a kind of stage—was hired for the occasion, and on the stage stood a good-sized table, supplied with pens, ink, and paper, and surrounded by eight stout chairs—one for each councillor. By one o'clock "the trusted of the people" had all arrived and taken their seats with countenances carefully arranged, to suit the solemnity of the occasion which had called them together. Some interested ratepayers occupied the body of the hall, and watched the proceedings of the "trusted ones" with awe and admiration.

The first business to be transacted was the appointment of a chairman. Two councillors were proposed for the office, and there were four votes for each. Here was a dilemma—a deadlock. What was to be done? A gruff voice from among the audience was heard to exclaim, "Toss up for it!" a proposition rightly met by a volley of indignant and withering looks from the councillors.

After a short pause, a remarkably solemn looking councillor moved that the "County Council Act" be consulted, with a view to finding a way out of the difficulty. This motion being duly carried, the County's Act was produced, and a clause eventually discovered bearing on the matter, and which stated that lots were to be drawn by some totally disinterested individual. It was naturally felt that it would be extremely undignified on the part of a councillor to go and hunt up a suitable party. Still somebody must undertake the duty —the two embryo chairmen and their supporters could not sit staring blankly at one another all day—the county work would never be got through in that fashion, nor the county roads ever graded and metalled. At this crisis a gentleman among the audience—all honour to him—volunteered to find an eligible person, and on his offer being graciously accepted, rushed from the hall. He first encountered a workman halfway up a ladder, standing against a building in course of erection, and called out to him to come and draw lots for the chairmanship of the county. The man on the ladder, owing probably to the hammering that was going on, evidently only imperfectly heard, for instead of replying, he hailed his mate on the roof with a "Hi, Bill! here is a go. They wants me to go and be chairman of the county." Bill leant over the parapet, and delivered himself as follows—"You take my tip, Jack, and have nothing to do with 'em!" and this advice Jack concluded to follow, and refused to be beguiled from his ladder. Nothing daunted, however, the public-spirited volunteer proceeded with his search, and after a considerable lapse of time, returned with a small boy in charge, whom he triumphantly marched up the hall, amid murmurs of applause.

In the meantime the only "bell-topper" to be

MEETING OF THE COUNTY COUNCIL.

found among the head-gear of the assembled sages had been called into requisition, placed in position on the table, and the names of the proposed chairmen written on pieces of paper and laid in it.

The boy was now commanded to approach the hat and draw. At this supreme moment the scene was most impressive. Round about, in various attitudes, betokening the deep interest they felt in the proceedings, were the eight councillors, and on tiptoes in front of the table was the small boy, endeavouring amid profound silence to fathom the depths of the bell-topper. Never before had that small boy in the course of his brief life been such an object of interest outside his own family. The eyes of the leading men in the county were on him, and the election of chairman of the County Council was in his hands. It ought to have been a proud moment for that lad, but I regret to record he hardly seemed duly impressed.

At last his not too nimble fingers secured one of the pieces of paper, the boy became once more an insignificant atom of humanity in flour-bag pants, and the selected chairman was duly announced. He assumed the position with a calm dignity and solemnity, which seemed to proclaim him as not being unaccustomed to such honours, and the County Council proceeded to business.

The Supreme Moment.*

The practical working of this system is not at present very satisfactory, and the last half-yearly

* In order to avoid the possibility of giving offence, I have taken care not to caricature any actual members of the Council.

statement of accounts shows that the roads of the district were not so economically managed as when they were under the former Road Boards, which did not involve the keeping up of this august body, the County Council.

CHAPTER XXVII.

CONCLUSION.

At the commencement of this narrative, I expressed my opinion that persons fond of outdoor amusements, and with moderate incomes, would get on very well in New Zealand. Four or five hundred a year is thought little of at home, but a gentleman out here with such an income, would be deemed a man of very considerable importance, and if he felt an inclination for politics, would have little difficulty in securing a seat in the House of Representatives.

These are the kind of men the colony wants—men who would take up politics for the good of their adopted country, and not for the sake of an honorarium which the country cannot afford to pay.

New Zealand has now passed the pioneer stage, and, like a newly built and furnished hotel, is prepared to receive any amount of visitors, but they must bring their cheque books with them. She has all the necessaries of ordinary civilised life, plenty of labour, cities lit with gas and the electric light, churches, houses furnished with bath-rooms and hot and cold water pipes, clubs, hotels, railways, telephones, roads, carriages, tramways, steamships, yachts, billiard rooms, and her big dock in Auckland, which Mr. Froude laughs at in " Oceana."

Now I cannot resist saying a word or two about this part of his book.

Mr. Froude seems annoyed with the citizens of Auckland for the improvements they are carrying out, particularly with the dock, and predicts that New Zealand will never grow into a new nation thus.

I don't for a moment presume to dispute Mr. Froude's judgment with regard to the baneful effect likely to be produced by a big dock on a young colony; it is a subject I have never studied, and I have no intention of pitting my opinion against his. Still, *humanum est errare*, and Mr. Froude, though an historian, is human, and in this particular instance, most colonials in the province of Auckland think mistaken as well, as he certainly is with regard to the harbour and the dimensions of the dock. Referring to them, he says: "Public works form the excuse for the borrowing, and there are works enough and to spare in progress. They are laying out a harbour, cutting down half a hillside in the process, suited for the ambitious Auckland that is to be, but ten times larger than there is present need of. They are excavating the biggest graving dock in the world (the *Great Eastern* would float in it with ease), preparing for the fleets, which are to make Auckland their headquarters."

I am utterly at a loss to know what Mr. Froude means by saying they are laying out a harbour, as Auckland harbour has been laid out by nature, and man has had no hand in it. A part of the foreshore has certainly been reclaimed within the last three or four years, and on the reclaimed land now stands the Auckland railway terminus, the Auckland Freezing Company's premises, some large flour mills, an hotel, and some other buildings. To fill in this reclamation, they utilised a precipitous hill, overshadowing the main road from Parnell to Auckland, which was slipping, and in a highly dangerous condition; but how can that be called "laying out a harbour"? The hill had to be removed, as part actually slipped one morning, carried away a building, and fell across the road, nearly burying an omnibus and its contents.

Does Mr. Froude blame the Harbour Board for converting this dangerous hillside into valuable building land?

With regard to dimensions, the new Auckland dock, "The Calliope" (which Mr. Froude calls the biggest in the world), is 500 feet long. There are two docks, I believe, at Birkenhead, each 750 feet long; two at Plymouth, each 644 feet long; one now in course of construction in Sydney, N.S.W., 630 feet long; one at Carleton, N.B., 630 feet long; and one at Liverpool, 501 feet long. The *Great Eastern* steamship is one of the two vessels afloat that will *not fit* in the Calliope dock.

So much for Mr. Froude's facts about the dimensions of the dock. Now a word about the wisdom of having made it.

Auckland harbour is, without question, one of the best natural harbours in the universe. Its depth is so great that ships can enter at any state of the tide. A channel a mile wide, and so perfectly clear of obstacles that the services of the pilot are often dispensed with, leads to its entrance, which is snugly sheltered by outlying islands. Its coaling facilities are magnificent, the supply of coal inexhaustible, and its position with regard to the groups of islands forming the eastern portion of the continent of Australasia, must render it, I should think, a desirable point for a naval station. All it required to make it perfect was a dock of sufficient dimensions to take in any of Her Majesty's ships of war, and hence the big dock. If Auckland is ever utilised as a naval station, immense benefit must accrue to the town. A man of war or two, with six or seven hundred hands apiece, means a good many hundred pounds' worth of business a week to the tradesmen of Auckland. But Mr. Froude says this sort of thing will never make New Zealand a nation. He thinks the people should go and live in the country, raise crops, breed sheep and cattle, and not bother about towns and big docks. Surely he forgets that the farmer must have a market, and that his prosperity depends on the demand for his produce, and therefore in a great measure on the prosperity of the towns.

A few more words, and I will have said my say. I trust the reader will pardon all my shortcomings, and will bear in mind that I have only endeavoured to describe my own experiences in the colony, my own impression concerning matters that have come under my notice, and some opinions I have gathered from old colonials. I know nothing of agricultural pursuits, but believe that the kind of farming most suitable to this part of the colony is sheep-farming, my principal reasons for so thinking being that many of the Kaiparians appear to do well at it, and that a Matakohe resident, our local J.P., carries off nearly every year two or three prizes for sheep at the Annual Show held in Auckland, and last year the first prize for Shropshires. Grapes do splendidly in this district, and I think wine-making will one day become a leading industry. The olive also grows remarkably well, and I fancy I see another industry sticking out in that direction. Our mineral resources have never been tapped, though there are many indications of hidden wealth.

The colony is undoubtedly passing through a period of depression (in which it is by no means singular), and is suffering as well from too much government, both local and general. It however still possesses plenty of vitality, and only wants time, and men earnest for its good, at the head of affairs, to nurse it into a vigorous and flourishing condition.

At the present, indeed, it offers little inducement to professional men, to endeavour to pursue their callings, but what better time, when land is so cheap, could be selected by gentlemen with small fixed incomes to come out, and purchase properties. I should strongly advise family men to bring if possible their own servants with them, and to get an agreement signed immediately on reaching Auckland, binding them, on consideration of the passage money, to remain a certain time in their service at certain wages. I cannot help thinking that there are many at home with moderate incomes who would do far better out here, and who could become important personages in New Zealand if they chose to take up public matters. They must, however, as I mentioned before, be people who like a free and easy life, untrammelled by stiff rules of society. The climate of the North Island is said to be all that can be desired for those whom a tropical life has unsuited to endure the harsh winds, the fogs, and the cold of England; and although I have not travelled the colony sufficiently to feel competent to pass an opinion as to which are the most desirable localities, still I do not think I can be wrong in mentioning as a summer or autumn retreat the Northern Kaipara.

THE END.

www.ingramcontent.com/pod-product-compliance
Lightning Source LLC
Chambersburg PA
CBHW021834230426
43669CB00008B/972